RENEWAL
for Field Leaders
Leading Your Direct Selling Team
Back to Growth

Brett A. Blake

Author of

RENEWAL: Leading Direct Selling Turnarounds, and

Private Equity Investing in Direct Selling: Identifying Risks

& Rewards

RENEWAL for Field Leaders: Leading Your Direct Selling Team Back to Growth
© 2020 Brett A. Blake. All rights reserved.

ISBN-13: 978-1-7333568-4-8

Contents

Introduction: Going South—*Learning the Leadership Lessons of Renewal* 1

Chapter 1: Defying Gravity—*An Industry with a Clear Pattern*..............8

Chapter 2: A Tale of Two Tails—*Failure to Renewal vs. Failure to Renew* 20

Chapter 3: Seeing Around Corners—*Anticipating Slower Growth or Sales Declines* 26

Chapter 4: The Renewal C.H.I.S.E.L.—*Six Variables Every Renewal Plan Should Include* 36

Chapter 5: Cash—*The Oxygen of Your Business* 43

Chapter 6: Hope—*Fuel for the Field* 51

Chapter 7: Innovation—*A Field Leader's Guide* 70

Chapter 8: Simplify—*Removing Layers to Discover the Core*............103

Chapter 9: Expanding to New Markets—*Finding New Customers in New Places* 117

Chapter 10: Leading During Tough Times—*Being Present and Positive*...126

Chapter 11: Beyond Your C.H.I.S.E.L.—*Other Considerations That Impact Pace* 136

Chapter 12: When You Fail to Renew—*Other Options When Growth Doesn't Happen* 140

Acknowledgments..150

About the Author 151

RENEWAL for Field Leaders

Introduction: Going South—*Learning the Leadership Lessons of Renewal*

Leadership and learning are indispensable to each other.
~ John F. Kennedy

It wasn't my first international trip, but it was my first time flying international first class, and the first time I had been excited about flying United Airlines (I was a Delta frequent flyer). The experience was far superior to any flight I had taken in my previous 33 years, and I was impressed, not with the drinks (I don't drink) and not with the food (it was almost midnight and I wasn't hungry) but with the lay-flat beds, thick blanket and personal pillow I was issued. My sleep was sound, the 14-hour flight was short, and I landed in Sydney in time to make it to my new office for my first day.

Despite the restful flight, jet lag got the best of me when I tried to make a left-hand turn in downtown Sydney and suddenly found myself in a very awkward situation. All of the parked cars and those coming my way seemed to be heading the wrong direction. I was sure they had all made a mistake until my mind broke through the fog, and I realized I was on the wrong side of the road *and* going the wrong way on a one-way street. I had no choice but to back up into the busy intersection, regain my bearings and continue to my hotel—this time on the left side of the road and going with the flow of traffic.

I had been sent to Australia for an indefinite period of time to address an urgent business crisis for our direct selling company and to right-size a division that was hemorrhaging cash and had seen sales drop from nearly $50 million to just $25 million. The crisis resulted in three lawyers (one hired by the previous general manager, one hired by the current general manager and the last by our then-marketing manager).

After a shower, I drove to the office to interview the current management and to dive into the economics of the subsidiary. My interviews didn't lead to new discoveries but gave me a firsthand account of what I had been told before. The previous general manager had been let go on account of the free-fall in sales and the lack of a plan to address the decline. His predecessor had been on the job for less than a month when a senior manager accused him of sexual harassment and therefore needed to be replaced. All of that was widely known, but what was not clear until these interviews was the fact that the marketing manager was not prepared or capable of making a meaningful contribution to the company's turnaround.

Just before retiring for bed that first night in Sydney, I called the home office in the United States to inform them that I had arrived and concluded that we had to fire the marketing manager as well.

Within the week, I had created and executed a plan to bring the employee base in-line with current sales, but what I thought would be the end of crisis management mode was only the beginning. By the end of the first month we would face three additional crises. The first was a story aired by the Australian Broadcasting Corporation (ABC) about a man who had called himself a doctor but had no medical credentials. In the B-roll or background footage of that news story they ran images of our company's products, clearly leading viewers to believe this man was associated with us. He wasn't. The second was the news that the new skincare line we were set to launch the following month at a series of live events had sold out in the U.S. We would not be able to have product for our markets (Australia and New Zealand) for three to six months. And finally, as if those other issues weren't bad enough, we received a letter threatening a lawsuit over our products.

Over the next six months we would resolve all legal matters for less than $10K, we would demand and receive an on-air and written apology from ABC, and we would see steady growth in sales from month two and beyond. I left the country within six months having hired a new general manager of subsidiaries that were profitable and growing.

None of this success would have been possible if it weren't for the field leaders who partnered with me in weekly calls to discuss our plan of action and then went to work leading their teams. I left Australia knowing that Renewal was possible no matter the circumstances and the rate of Renewal increases dramatically when field leaders are engaged in the process as equal partners.

This experience would be the beginning of a career working with companies and field leaders in need of Renewal. While I can't claim a 100% success rate, I'm proud of the condition I left each of the companies in. One of them should not have survived but did. Another found a large corporate buyer. Another that had declined more than 40% before my arrival had rebounded to within 1% of the previous year's sales by the time I left, and two achieved long-term growth leading to total annual sales of more than $1 billion each.

As is the case in many experiences in life, I've learned critical lessons in each of the above circumstances. In fact, I probably learned more from the not so successful experiences than from those that were true turnarounds. But it didn't occur to me that my experience would be valuable to others until I had stepped away from the day-to-day work. It took time away from an operating role and the chance to connect with CEOs and executives running companies in need of Renewal before all of the lessons learned came together in a system that I believe can be followed by any direct selling leader. In fact, I didn't realize how common the need for Renewal was until I completed the research necessary to record and graph the sales of dozens of direct selling companies for another book I wrote.[1] During that research I came to understand that every direct selling company has gone through a period of Renewal. Even the most successful have had at least one period of declining sales. The oldest and most successful have experienced multiple periods of Renewal.

While the great companies have experienced decline and found a way to renew growth, there are plenty of examples of companies that have experienced declines and never returned to growth... or even worse, have continued to decline—some until they were claimed by bankruptcy, sold to one of the firms creating conglomerates from the remnants of failed or failing companies, changed channels or closed their doors. We lament the stars of yesteryear that are gone now, like Longaberger[2], and

---

[1] *Private Equity Investing in Direct Selling: Identifying Risks and Rewards*
[2] Longaberger did announce an attempt to relaunch starting with QVC just as we were preparing to publish the first edition of this book.

those that have become a much smaller version of their past selves, like Pampered Chef and Creative Memories.

RENEWAL for Field Leaders: Leading Your Direct Selling Team Back to Growth presents an inventory of the variables field leaders should understand about the process of Renewal and provides specific suggestions to help field leaders improve the probability of success with their own business.

I do believe that a company is more likely to experience Renewal more quickly if field leaders understand their role in leading during challenging times. Ideally, field leaders and corporate executives will both understand the variables taught in this book and its companion *RENEWAL: Leading Direct Selling Turnarounds*. However, even if your corporate executive team is not actively implementing these variables, I believe field leaders can employ the variables taught to improve things for their team.

This book offers a set of variables to consider when the company you represent has a downturn in sales and needs to renew growth. These variables—especially your leadership (that and a little bit of luck) will be your key to growth. Your commitment to reading and understanding "what you should do" is a critical first step and is evidence that you have the humility to admit that the things you've been doing during your period of growth (or Hyper-Growth) won't be the answer to *renewing* growth. In the end, applying your learning and leading with courage will be the enabling factors in your team's success.

RENEWAL for Field Leaders

Chapter 1: Defying Gravity—*An Industry with a Clear Pattern*

There is no such thing as a company that grows forever without eventually hitting the wall, or at least slowing down to go over a speed bump.
~ Ron Ashkenas, *Harvard Business Review*

By the time I decided to leave Beachbody so I could move closer to my mom who was battling life-threatening cancer, I was certain I knew how to be successful in direct selling. I had started my career at Melaleuca and rode their wave from just above $20 million in sales to $105 million and left just after we reached $210 million. I joined USANA during a period of decline and after the board gave me the chance to craft and implement a strategy, the company began to grow again (and has seen steady growth every year for more than 15 years). When I arrived at Beachbody, its direct selling division—Team Beachbody—was in decline. It had grown to approximately $50 million on the back of an infomercial referral program, but when the economics of their model forced them to pull the plug on that program, the division's sales dropped. When I arrived in January of 2010, Team Beachbody was producing just a bit more than $3 million a month and several top leaders were considering "full-time jobs." As GM of that division, I was proud of the fact that we would close 2013 at just under $400 million in sales.

I'll be the first to admit that I had very little to do with the success of these three companies, but having lived and breathed each experience, I was fairly certain I understood how to grow and regrow network marketing companies. However, I was about to learn of the truth of behavioral scientist Daniel Kahneman's conclusion that "declarations of high confidence mainly tell you that an individual has constructed a coherent story in his mind, not necessarily that the story is true." [3]

I left an operating role at Beachbody and joined their Board of Directors and took a job as the CEO of a very small party-plan company called Jewel Kade. I accepted the job in part because it allowed me to move close to my mom, in part because it allowed

---

[3] Daniel Kahneman, *Thinking, Fast and Slow* (New York: Farrar, Straus & Giroux), 2013.

me to avoid competing with Beachbody and the field leaders I cared about, and also because I recognized that party-plan companies tend to hit a wall as they grow. My confidence (or arrogance) led me to conclude that I could actually help solve that problem, not only at Jewel Kade but for other party-plan companies as well.

During the next several years, first at Jewel Kade and then at Origami Owl, I would learn that applying tactics with success at one company didn't always lead to success at another. I recognized how easy it is to exaggerate our own importance—or even the importance of knowledge and skill—and to underestimate the role of luck and chance.

While I'm extraordinarily proud of the work we did and the outcomes at both Jewel Kade (sold to Thirty-One Gifts) and Origami Owl (returned to the owners with a bright future today), neither of those companies has experienced the same record of sales growth I've seen at other companies.

The learning and humility gained at both of these party-plan companies and a short tenure at AdvoCare helped me to reflect on the key variables a CEO must focus on when presented with a decline in their business.

I don't believe that every company can be saved. I don't believe that great leadership is the only key to turning sales around. Companies are dynamic and face millions of outside influences that can impact success or failure. Competition, market trends, social media algorithms, distributor claims, supply chain integrities and even weather can impact a company's results. As Kahneman puts it:

> *Narrative fallacies arise inevitably from our continuous attempt to make sense of the world. The explanatory stories that people find compelling are simple; are concrete rather than abstract; assign a larger role to talent, stupidity, and intentions than to luck; and focus on a few striking events that happened rather than on the countless events that failed to happen. Any recent salient event is a candidate to become the kernel of a causal narrative. Taleb suggests that we humans constantly fool ourselves by constructing flimsy accounts of the past and believing they are true.[4]*

"Countless events" can contribute to success or failure, but I believe that failure is certain if leaders don't understand and address key variables during a downturn. The variables I will introduce to you in this book are not an elixir, but I do believe that ignoring them will guarantee failure. The "C.H.I.S.E.L." variables I describe later in this book will provide field leaders

---

[4] Ibid.

like you context to understand the essential building blocks your company's executive team will focus on to renew growth, and provide you the guidance you need to make sure you and your team survive the inevitable downturn.

Yes, I said "inevitable downturn."

Your Business Will Experience No Growth, Slow Growth and a Decline

Believe it or not, your company is not destined to continuous and unencumbered growth. At least among direct selling companies, history tells a narrative of three to five years of Hyper-Growth followed by a few years of no growth or decline. How the company and its field leaders respond to the period of decline will determine whether it will continue or be replaced with renewed growth.

To illustrate my point, I have included a visual chart showing six direct selling companies that went through rapid growth, decline and found renewed growth. It's true that most of these companies are public (it's difficult to get reliable information on private companies that can be published), but my experience tells me that every private company that undergoes similar Hyper-Growth will also go through a time of retraction.

Nu Skin

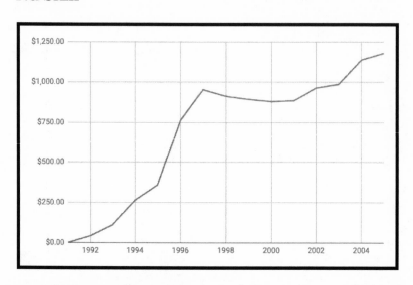

USANA Health Sciences

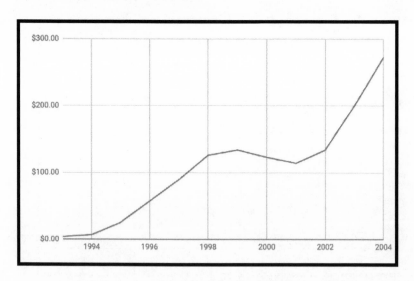

Scentsy

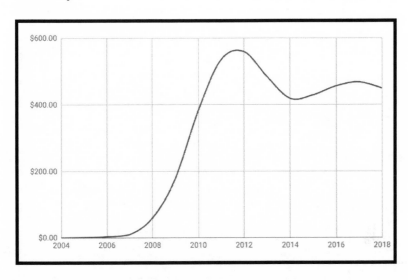

Thirty-One Gifts

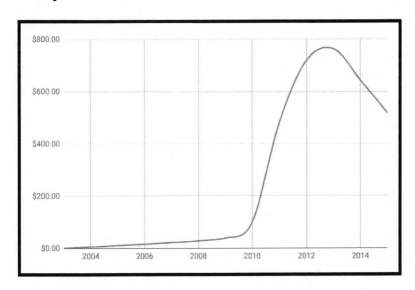

Arbonne International

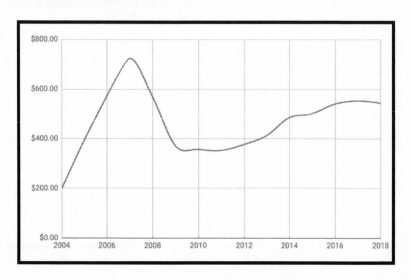

Natura

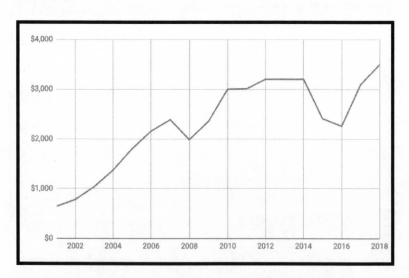

All of these examples show companies that were able to regain traction, and a few had sustainable sales for many years after their initial decline. The data to which I've had access leads me to believe that there is something about direct selling companies that makes it historically impossible to sustain rapid growth in the early years without experiencing a flattening or decline later.

Why do direct sales companies fail to sustain growth year after year? One of the theories for the decline after years of strong growth is that these companies' sales outpace the development of field leaders to support the number of distributors recruited. That is why I felt it so important to write this guide for field leaders.

Because of the channel's dependence on volunteer sales and organically acquired field leadership, often revenues tend to overtake a company's ability to grow the field leadership. Author Eric Worre teaches that most companies can only grow leadership at a rate of 10% per year, and sales growth above that rate forewarns future declines. In an interview I had with LifeVantage CEO Darren Jensen, he described this challenge:

> *Too many investors are attracted by a company in the "pop phase" not knowing that as a rule of thumb it will only run for eighteen months or so, and then there's a one hundred percent probability that the company will either implode or that they*

will go through a glide or flat phase. They will see a flattening of the business or a slow downward glide while the underlying distributor leadership base catches up with the revenue.

Subscribers to Worre's leadership sustainability theory argue that sales will continue to decline or remain flat until they reach a level the field leaders can manage—either via declining sales or increasing leadership.

"The key is to understand that a slowing, flattening and often a downward glide in sales is a predictable reaction to significant sales growth," Jensen added.

The purpose of this book is not to diagnose the cause or to suggest preventative action. I don't pretend to have a valid theory for either. Instead, the goal of this book is to prepare field leaders for a reversal, to help them recognize the problem early, and to give them a tool kit for responding and renewing their team's growth.

Knowing that no direct selling company will have continuous uninterrupted sales growth should be both frightening and comforting to field leaders. It should leave you with a sobering expectation that the work in front of you may not always be about playing catch-up. It should also help those of you who have experienced a spike followed by a fall to forgive yourselves and not take the results so personally or even worse to blame your corporate executive team. A downward slide is not always a sign of poor leadership. Corrections happen, but whether they prove to be little bumps in the road or a continuously declining experience for your team can be influenced by the decisions you make and your ability to focus on all the right things.

My goal is to equip you to make all the right decisions by helping you see the spectrum of variables that need your attention during a time of Renewal. But before I introduce you to the "C.H.I.S.E.L." variables, I want to share two true tales of companies that experienced declining sales and the dramatic difference in the end result for each.

Chapter 2: A Tale of Two Tails—*Failure to Renewal vs. Failure to Renew*

The illusion that one has understood the past feeds the further illusion that one can predict and control the future. These illusions are comforting. They reduce the anxiety that we would experience if we allowed ourselves to fully acknowledge the uncertainties of existence. We all have a need for the reassuring message that actions have appropriate consequences, and that success will reward wisdom and courage. Many business books are tailor-made to satisfy this need.
~ Daniel Kahneman, *Thinking, Fast and Slow*

Dave Longaberger and Mark Hughes both founded and led a direct selling company to national prominence during their lifetime. Both had struggled in school. Mark dropped out in the

9th grade before being compelled to return to a school for troubled students. Dave stuck with it but was held back in the first grade, forced to repeat 5th grade twice, and didn't graduate from high school until he was 21. Both Dave and Mark were beloved by the distributors in the companies they founded. They died about one year apart—Mark at age 44 and Dave at age 64.

While Dave and Mark had many things in common, their reputations as CEOs of the companies they founded were actually vastly different. Dave came from a large family in the Midwest and built a company selling baskets he had learned to build from his father and grandfather. Mark grew up an only child with a single mother near Los Angeles and his company was built to sell weight loss supplements. While both companies used the direct selling channel, each sold with its own twist on compensating and selling (party-plan vs. network marketing). Dave built a "family" company from a small town in Southeast Ohio while Mark was a solo entrepreneur who built a company that flaunted the stereotypical Hollywood lifestyle.

Dave was the talk at all direct selling association meetings and was a darling of the government and media in Ohio. As his company grew, he hired more and more homegrown employees and built a corporate headquarters in the shape of a basket (the company's core product line) with its own public golf course. To the outside world, Dave's basket company, Longaberger, was built to last. It employed no "get rich quick" selling tactics and focused on rewarding product sales to end consumers. Not only that, but Dave and his company were model citizens.

Mark's company, Herbalife, couldn't have been more different. No one would accuse Mark of building a family company, in part because Mark had no family to build his company with or around, and in part because he displayed an openly rebellious streak. Herbalife faced actions from the Federal Drug Administration, the California State Attorney General, the California State Department of Health, the Department of Justice of Canada, two Herbalife distributors and company shareholders. Mark took on Congress with a brashness rarely seen in those hallowed halls when the federal government made moves to regulate nutritional supplements. The *LA Times* reported that "a U.S. Senate subcommittee called Hughes before a hearing in May. Referring to a panel of nutrition experts who had criticized Herbalife in testimony the previous day, he asked the senators, 'If they're such experts in weight loss, why were they so fat?'"[5]

Herbalife grew quickly and profitably in its first few years, but when it received so much negative press from government probes, it began to retract. Even when sales began to grow again in the 1990s, many believed that the company was a house of cards that someday would implode and self-destruct.

---

[5] https://www.latimes.com/archives/la-xpm-2000-may-22-me-32795-story.html accessed August 1, 2019.

And then tragedy struck both companies. Dave Longaberger was diagnosed with kidney cancer and died less than a year later on March 17, 1999. Mark Hughes had no time to prepare. On May 20, 2000 he was found dead in his Malibu beach house of an apparent accidental overdose.[6]

Two direct selling founders, dead. Two successful companies with sales around one billion dollars, both starting over without their enthusiastic founders.

In the immediate aftermath of the founders' deaths, Longaberger's and Herbalife's sales reacted differently. Herbalife began a slow decline while Longaberger's sales continued to grow reaching a billion dollars in annual sales the year of Dave's death. Had experts been told at the time that one of these companies would become one of the world's largest direct sellers and the other would fail, most would have predicted Longaberger as the winner and Herbalife the loser. That prediction wouldn't have been more wrong.

Twenty years later, we are left to contemplate two very different results. Anyone with access to Google or a cursory knowledge of today's direct selling companies will know that Longaberger and Herbalife defied the public opinion of their time. Herbalife has grown to become a top five direct selling

---

[6] https://web.archive.org/web/20130313003715/http://articles.cnn.com/2000-06-17/us/hughes.death_1_accidental-overdose-final-autopsy-results-malibu-mansion?_s=PM%3AUS, accessed November 5, 2019.

company in sales and has created billions of dollars of value for public shareholders. On the opposite tail of our tale, Longaberger is gone. After Dave's death, Longaberger experienced a sudden surge of sales and then slowly and steadily declined until it was sold to a company that became insolvent. The basket shaped headquarters stands in disrepair—a sad symbol of what might have been.

The stories of these two companies represent extreme examples of what is possible when direct selling companies face adversity. A company's history isn't a good predictor of its future. These examples prove the truth of the first half of Winston Churchill's famous maxim: "Success is not final" and the fallacy of the second half: "Failure is not fatal." Failure can, in fact, be fatal. Herbalife found a way to turn what many believed was certain failure into Renewal, then growth and long-term success. Longaberger rode a wave of short-term success, but when the wave subsided management failed to take the necessary steps to renew their opportunity and suffered the complete loss of their utopia-like company.

Lessons Learned

I chose to include the stories of these two companies to remind you of the potential—both good and bad—for a company that begins to experience a decline. Herbalife and Longaberger are not alone at their respective tail ends of this tale of two companies. There are several examples of companies that have experienced signs of failure yet found a way to renew growth, as well as several examples of companies with continued decline and others that have experienced complete failure.

Momentum matters in direct selling, especially when it comes to recruiting others to connect their hopes and dreams to your company's products and opportunity, but momentum can be changed. Field leaders should be clear that momentum in either direction is not permanent. No company has experienced never-ending growth and no company has to experience perpetual decline. Leadership matters and you can make a difference in impacting both sides of momentum. Our focus in the coming chapters will be to provide field leaders a set of variables that must be considered and proactively managed as part of their team's plan for Renewal. Those with companies still in growth will also benefit from a study of these variables by learning what NOT to do and how to avoid making changes that needlessly stall your team's growth.

Let's begin by making sure you're keeping your eye on the Key Performance Indicators (KPIs) that will forewarn sales declines, and then introduce you to the variables that must be part of your Renewal plan.

Chapter 3: Seeing Around Corners—
Anticipating Slower Growth or Sales Declines

*It's not that we can predict bubbles—if we could,
we would be rich. But we can certainly have a
bubble warning system.*
~ Richard Thayer, American Economist

At 7:02 a.m. December 7, 1941, volunteer George Elliott was practicing with new radar equipment that had been set up recently on the Opana, a knoll in the foothills of Oahu, Hawaii, when he detected incoming aircraft. The equipment that was installed as a warning system to help protect Pearl Harbor worked just as it should. Unfortunately, they were not able to warn the fleet at Pearl Harbor because when Elliott and his working companion, Joseph Lockard, called in to report what they saw to their superior, Lt. Kermit Tyler, Tyler "reasoned that the radar blip was a flight of Army B-17 bombers due in that morning. Lt. Tyler instructed the Opana Radar operations to disregard the information and not to worry about it."[7]

At 7:53 a.m., the first of two waves of Japanese aircraft attacked Pearl Harbor. Elliott and Lockard had closed up the radar center after being reassured that what they had seen were American aircraft, and they didn't find out what they had missed until after breakfast that morning. That morning "2,403 Americans were killed and 1,143 were wounded. Eighteen ships were sunk or run aground, including five battleships"[8] in a Japanese attack on Pearl Harbor.

I'm surprised how often direct selling companies have similar—though fortunately not fatal—experiences when they see signs that should sound an alarm for their company. Instead of heeding the warnings and taking the appropriate actions, too many companies ignore or brush aside the data with a false confidence that they are signs that need not be responded to. In this chapter, we will provide a reminder of the early warning signs that the direction of sales is about to change.

---

[7] https://npgallery.nps.gov/NRHP/GetAsset/NHLS/91001379_text, accessed August 10, 2019.

[8] https://en.wikipedia.org/wiki/Attack_on_Pearl_Harbor accessed August 10, 2019

What Goes UP...

Those who have studied the direct selling industry will recognize that there is a preponderance of evidence proving that direct selling companies do not continue to grow at double-digit rates forever. However, during times of double-digit growth, it's easy to ignore the evidence and perhaps even believe that you have stumbled upon something no other company before you has figured out: how to grow forever. To be fair, even rational leaders who understand that their growth won't last forever sometimes are so consumed with their company's meteoric growth that they don't have the bandwidth to consider the possibility that their growth may someday slow and/or decline.

I suspect that if I had the opportunity to interview every leader whose company has seen sales slow and decline, they'd say they would have paid millions to have received advanced warning that their momentum was about to change. Yet, the experience of nearly every company in the industry would lead any objective thinker to conclude that sales growth never continues uninterrupted, and therefore every company should have an advanced warning system in place to help them see around the proverbial corner.

Waiting until sales start to slow or decline is too late. Leaders need to be prepared to respond *before* they actually see the enemy overhead.

29

Business Lifecycle Stages

Before we introduce you to an advanced warning system of sorts, let's first remind you of business lifecycle theory and define the stages of a company's life. Several individuals and institutions have their own version of the stages of a company, but I have chosen to define my own stages of a direct selling company and have based my model on a non-direct selling theory taught by The Corporate Finance Institute.[9] I believe understanding that all companies are susceptible to common lifecycle stages will help you to be less defensive about your company's transition from one stage to the next, and perhaps leave you more open to preparing for each stage so that you can make the necessary changes to extend your company's life and ensure Renewal rather than long-term decline.

I believe that direct selling companies experience the following lifecycle stages:

- **Launch**
- **Hyper-Growth**
- **Growth by Promotion**
- **Shake-Out**
- **Decline or Renewal**

---

[9] https://corporatefinanceinstitute.com/resources/knowledge/finance/business-life-cycle/, accessed November 5, 2019.

Stages in the Lifecycle of a Direct Selling Company

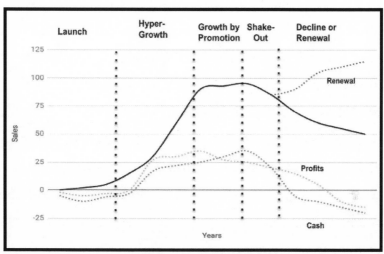

© by Brett A. Blake

Lifecycle Stage 1: Launch

During the Launch stage, a company is figuring out its product, marketing, field compensation and selling systems. The Launch phase is marked by losses in both profits and cash as companies often use investor dollars or debt to fund operations. In direct selling, the Launch phase can be months or years depending on how long it takes to figure out selling systems that work and to recruit field leaders who are capable of exploiting those selling systems to grow the company.

Lifecycle Stage 2: Hyper-Growth

Hyper-Growth quickly puts companies in the black with growing profits and plenty of cash, though not cash available for distribution. During this phase, cash generated by the business is often consumed almost entirely by needed capital investment and inventory purchases to keep up with the growth. The chart above shows a positive cash flow, but a few companies experience so much growth that they are unable to fund growth from operating cash and are required to borrow to keep up. Nevertheless, their growth is so compelling that they rarely have difficulty in finding vendors (if not lenders) to help meet their need for cash. In other words, cash, whether from operations or from willing investors, is available and deployed quickly.

Lifecycle Stage 3: Growth by Promotion

During the Growth by Promotion stage, the company continues to grow, but that growth requires much more effort and expense. Companies get more aggressive with promotions, increase the number and frequency of product launches, and spend more and more on promotions to continue to grow. The pace of growth peaks during this stage before beginning to slow.

Because the company's growth no longer requires significant investment in infrastructure and inventory, companies in the Growth by Promotion stage have more cash available for distributions than at any previous stage. Cash is plentiful, but profits and margins are declining on a relative basis as sales growth is driven by margin constraining promotions and/or new product introductions.

As the lifecycle chart above illustrates, profits peak just as the company moves from the Hyper-Growth stage to the Growth by Promotion stage but interestingly enough, cash doesn't peak until late in the Growth by Promotion stage and often not until the company's sales are already headed toward decline.

Lifecycle Stage 4: Shake-Out

The Shake-Out stage is characterized by declining sales. During this phase, sales growth has not simply slowed, but sales are actually in decline. Often the first signs of a sales decline are attributed to seasonal slowing or a poor product launch. Missing the signs of decline can be costly because during the Shake-Out stage a company's cash position can change dramatically, often moving from peak cash production to a cash crisis within months.

I have labeled this phase the "Shake-Out" stage because it is during this time when a company will make the decisions and adaptations that will eventually lead them either toward Renewal and additional growth, or decline—too often rapid decline.

Lifecyle Stage 5: Decline or Renewal

During the Decline or Renewal stage the company either makes necessary changes to improve topline sales or they see cash move into negative territory and run out of options. The model above shows a dotted line for Renewal, but the profit and cash lines only show the results of continued decline.

Though not charted above, those companies that are attentive to the variables I will introduce in the chapters to follow will make significant operating improvements to their business. Therefore, when they are able to renew growth in topline sales, both their profit and cash positions rebound dramatically. Unless they enter Hyper-Growth again, the company returns to be a very healthy cash producer.

Advanced Warning Systems: Why Sales Aren't Enough

You might be asking, "Why do I need KPIs? Won't my sales be enough to signal trouble?" Perhaps, but not always. Sometimes sales can be a misleading KPI since many companies continue to have increasing sales (Growth by Promotion) even as the new customer/distributor count is declining (signaling declining sales in the future). For example, I interviewed one CEO of a direct selling company that had been the sweetheart of the channel. In that interview, he told me that his business had been in decline for more than a year before his team acknowledged that they were actually in trouble. This executive (who asked to remain nameless) said that his biggest regret was that he had ignored the signs of decline because sales had continued to climb even though new customer and distributor enrollments had fallen.

"I let the sales numbers fool me into thinking things were fine," he said. "I didn't realize until it was too late that the sales growth had shifted from more customers buying to fewer customers buying more."

For this CEO's company, sales had continued to grow because the company's average order size and the sales per distributor had increased. In other words, they were growing via promotions and more new products to existing customers. They were selling more product, but to fewer people. To make things worse, they were recruiting fewer new distributors and customers and so sales increased despite a shrinking distributor and customer base.

A Field Leader's Warning System

Most field leaders will be able to track the activity of their team. Field leaders should track three KPIs for their team:

- How many are ordering every month?
- How many are sponsoring?

- How many advancements do you have on your team each month?

Sometimes your numbers will fall from one month to the next, but when you see your numbers declining in one or more categories for three consecutive months, you have a problem that needs to be addressed. Note that the problem may be company-wide, or it might be an isolated issue with your team. While most teams decline when a company declines, there are almost always a few teams that continue to grow even while the bulk of the others are lagging. In other words, you can take action to make sure your team performs irrespective of the performance of other teams.

Chapter 4: The Renewal C.H.I.S.E.L.—*Six Variables Every Renewal Plan Should Include*

*Every block of stone has a statue inside it, and it is
the task of the sculptor to discover it.*
~ Michelangelo

The great Michelangelo understood that there was a masterpiece inside every block of stone, and he knew how to use his chisel to rid the statue of the excess material surrounding the work of art he wanted to reveal. Likewise, if your team has once known success, the answer to improved business performance likely can be found within the existing team, but it often requires leaders to chip away the excess programs, politics and promotions to find the company's compelling core and growth engine. The process is more art than science, but after years of experience in multiple operating and consulting assignments, I've found that there are a common set of variables that must be included in your plan. These variables combine to form the word C.H.I.S.E.L.—not the most visually aesthetic acronym, I'll admit, but the right variables to focus on if you're leading a turnaround.

I'll introduce you to the variables that make up your turnaround C.H.I.S.E.L. below and then we will talk about each in great detail in the chapters that follow. Here are the variables that require your attention if you are to renew your team's growth:

Cash

Hope

Innovation

Simplification

Expansion

Leadership

- **Cash**—While the C.H.I.S.E.L. variables are not meant to be sequential in order of importance, the first two variables are the most important because they serve as the fuel to power everything else you will want to do. Most of us have been taught that the goal for any business is to produce a profit. Amazon and dozens of successful technology companies have showed us that profits are eventually important, but the only thing that matters is the availability of cash. Simply put, cash is the fuel that allows a business to continue to operate, and during a downturn a business that previously had plenty of cash can find itself in a negative cash position in no time at all.

- **Hope**—If cash is a business's fuel, hope is the field's fuel. Without hope distributors stop recruiting, stop selling and start looking for something else to do with their time. Specifically, field sales representatives need to have hope that the company is the vehicle that will allow them to reach their dreams, and that means that it will be around and still in demand years from now. Often, companies that have a decline in sales, no matter how small, have field representatives who begin to weave and tell stories of long-term decline. These "leaders" and those who believe their stories no longer believe or have hope in their future with that company. Field leaders play an enormous role in preserving and renewing hope, and later we will talk about the things they can and should do to make sure they don't starve their teams of hope, or worse, that their words and actions don't drain hope from their team.

- **Innovation**—Any turnaround book will discuss innovation as a key ingredient of a Renewal plan. However, in direct selling, innovation too often is applied incorrectly and instead of contributing to Renewal, new products actually accelerate the decline. Too few companies understand that innovation is governed by a company's brand and the selling systems created to empower the field to acquire customers, distributors, and profitable leaders. Therefore, innovation can come in the form of brand renewal, system innovation, rewards and compensation innovation, technology innovation, or product innovation. Product innovation without thought to brand constraints or the system of selling the new product leads to confusion and can actually slow growth. Said more succinctly, if your selling system is designed to sell baskets, don't expect your field to be able to find Renewal if you introduce new jewelry without also introducing a new sales system to help them sell it.

Field leaders who understand the laws governing innovation can identify which products are actual growth engines, which are just there for extra volume and will realize some of the most important innovation can happen within your team.

- **Simplicity**—As companies grow and add more and more employees, the field begins to see more and more programs, products and promotions. At first all of this "new" is exciting. Adding to the complexity are field led programs and promotions that further complicate the business. Before long, so many initiatives, no matter how simple each one seems, become constraining and confusing to the field. As you prepare a plan for Renewal, deciding what *not* to do is sometimes as important as deciding what to do. Identifying what you will stop doing will also help you decide how to preserve cash.

- **Expansion**—While most non-direct sellers will point to new products as the primary driver of Renewal, for better or for worse the number one driver of Renewal in direct selling would have to be international expansion. While international expansion is easy to understand, there are opportunities and examples of companies expanding within their current country, finding pockets of growth in new states, new demographics or new languages. Just like new stores increase sales for brick-and-mortar retailers, new demographic and geographic expansion increases sales for direct sellers.

- **Leadership**—One of the interviews I recently had with the CEO of a company that has experienced a 70% decline in sales reminded me of this last critical variable that takes so much emotional energy to implement and too often is ignored. This critical variable of leadership is most often manifest in just being present for your team. Sometimes when things aren't going well and we feel like we don't have all the answers, we prefer to manage our business in solitary, to hunker down alone in our home office. Email, text and social media give us the illusion of effectively doing our job, but nothing substitutes for in-person communication and live reassurance from top field leaders. Most leaders were out in front and on the road constantly during their growth years, but they fail to continue that practice or to reimplement that behavior during their effort to renew their growth.

In times of crisis, leaders lead live.

Let's deep dive into each of the C.H.I.S.E.L. variables and give you both the understanding and tools you need to successfully lead your team to renewed growth.

Chapter 5: Cash—*The Oxygen of Your Business*

For better or worse, cash is the oxygen of your business, and you can't last long in any environment without it.
~ Neil Blumenthal, CEO Warby Parker

Most of us think that businesses live or die based on whether or not they are profitable. Turn a profit, live to see another day. Fail to turn a profit and you are done. That world view became outdated quickly in my family when my youngest brother asked me to invest in his first venture, "Know Marketing." Turns out that venture never came close to making a profit, but was transformed into Funding Universe, an idea that won $50,000 in a college entrepreneur contest and found angel investors who provided more capital until they merged with another company and changed the business model enough to attract more investor dollars. More than a decade later, the company, Lendio, is finally profitable and still raising money—now in the tens of millions of dollars. The lesson learned from watching Lendio is the same taught for decades by Amazon... you don't need to make a profit, but you'd better not run out of cash.

Cash Disappears in a Flash

Many field leaders who have never experienced a downturn don't understand why I would first focus on the need for cash—especially in a book written for field leaders. For most leaders in almost every stage of their business lifecycle, cash is so plentiful it's hard to imagine a scenario where they would need more.

Sudden changes in topline sales, is a cash account's worst nightmare. Often leaders that have experienced Hyper-Growth have allowed their personal spending to get out of control. They have team promotions and activities of every size and variety happening and have often purchased large homes or expensive cars—often with debt. None of these choices are an issue when their income was growing, but when sales begin to fall off and cash slows, it is surprising to see how often—and how quickly—the leader's cash position turns negative.

Whether you refer to it as fuel or oxygen or use a runway analogy, if you and your family have any hope of surviving a downturn and renewing growth, you will need time and money to figure things out. In my experience it often takes more than one small tweak to renew growth, so making sure you have cash on hand and some to spare must become your first and most urgent task. Too often, leaders deny that they are in decline or convince themselves that things will return to growth with just a little fine-tuning or a new product launch coming in a few months, so they delay making major cost cuts. Rarely does their optimism pay off. Instead they are forced to make more significant cost cuts or to take another job to ensure the family survives.

Before we review the formula for managing your personal cash, I want to acknowledge how difficult it is for top income earners to do anything that might signal to their team or to potential new recruits that they are not successful. Many believe that showing signs of wealth attracts others who want what you have. I assure you that there are many things you can do to scale back in a way that is not as visible (e.g. aligning with the company and not duplicating promotions, eliminating non-productive travel, educational and seminar expenses and subscriptions to online services). Some leaders will want to hire a professional who has worked with other direct sellers and will find an immediate ROI on the money spent (about $500 a month). Whatever you do, I can only encourage you not to wait. I assure you that the pain of not cutting expenses will far exceed any downside to signaling frugality to others.

Three-Step Formula for Cash Management

As soon as your early warning signals point to a downturn in sales, I recommend engaging in a simple three-step formula I call AIM. Focusing on this formula will help you do all you can to make sure there is plenty of cash to allow for Renewal. The formula is straightforward:

(1) **A**ccurately forecast your true cash position

(2) **I**dentify all sources of cash available

(3) **M**ake spending changes to free cash

Accurately Forecast Your True Cash Position

Most leaders have had no need to create and keep a personal budget. Many don't know how much they are spending each month or even what their "minimum income requirement" is to meet commitments to things like their mortgage.

Taking time to track your personal spending and to identify your cash needs is critical and will then allow you to create a forecast of how much you can save in the future.

If you begin to see any early warning signals that slower growth or declining sales are approaching, make sure you take time to create a forecast of your future income (checks/commissions) that is stripped of all optimism and 100% based on a trendline that reflects sales since the noted change in your early warning signals. Not only do you need a forecast of your income, but you also need to see an accurate cash forecast that includes the income trend and your anticipated spending based on your current spending. In other words, you need to know how much you will have left over in the months to come if your income continues to decline and your spending remains the same.

Identify Sources of Cash

Once you have a forecast of your personal cash position in the months to come, you need to identify any additional sources of cash you might be able to get if necessary. When most individuals think of the sources of cash available to them, they might include retirement savings like 401(k)s (if you are approaching retirement age), income from other work or by returning to work, or the least desirable and only a short-term solution, debt. However, for those who forecast their future cash needs early enough, they will have the best source of cash.

We can't talk about sources of cash without addressing the question that comes up most often when I'm talking with a field leader whose checks have gone down: "Should I take a full-time or part-time job?" The short answer is "YES!" "absolutely" and "for sure."

I understand the implications of taking a job and the message that it sends to your team but remember that your ability to continue supporting your team in the future depends on making sure you have the cash. You don't have to tell your team that you are taking a job because you don't believe in the company or even that your check is down. Surprisingly few will care and fewer will ask for an explanation and to those you can say "my team has gotten larger and I have more leaders to delegate to so, when this opportunity came I decided I could go back to work on my terms." You'll find your own language, and it is perfectly fine to tell your team—especially your leaders—that you've learned how important it is to make sure you have cash during downturns so you are being very conservative and taking a job now so you are certain to have the funds necessary to help your team get back on track.

Make Spending Changes to Free Cash

Wise leaders will begin to identify opportunities to reduce their monthly spending as soon as they see their income start to decline or even better as soon as their early warning signs show that a problem may be around the corner.

Cut Cost "Too Soon" and "Too Far" at First

My advice to leaders entering the Shake-Out stage is to make rapid and deep cuts to their spending as soon as possible. Too often, leaders make too few cuts too slowly. Review every opportunity to reduce your spending and, if necessary, engage the advice of a personal finance and budgeting professional.

"Nice to Have"

"Nice to have" things are the enemies of success. Cutting expenses will be painful and leaders need to have a survivor's mentality when reviewing the many, many good options that they will want to keep spending their money on. Sometimes it helps to remind yourself that leaders whose team experience Renewal will have the opportunity to return to a cash position that will allow some of these "nice to have" things to return. In the short-term, follow the mantra *When in doubt, do without.*

Support Your Company's Cost Cutting

Most of the time field leaders will not have a direct role to play in helping a company create or execute a plan to preserve cash, but smart field leaders support efforts management will make to be wise with the company's cash. When a direct selling company starts to make changes to preserve cash, the field most often is impacted in a way that is negative to them. For example, when you are expecting a catalog with ten new products and it comes out only having eight, it is easy to be disappointed. The field can get even more alarmed when the company that has been hiring for months or years suddenly begins to reduce its employee

51

count. Almost without exception, your team will begin to ask if the company "is going to make it."

Wise field leaders will look at management's efforts to preserve cash as a positive sign and will make sure that their team recognizes cuts as indications of good management. More troubling would be a company that ignores signs of decline with no visible efforts to cut back. Help your team understand how common it is for companies to have a correction after a cycle of growth. Your proactive communication during the Shake-Out stage can shorten its length and help get your company to Renewal more quickly. In my experience, the most significant challenge companies face during a period of decline is the challenge of convincing the field that their actions are sound business.

Chapter 6: Hope—*Fuel for the Field*

Optimism is the faith that leads to achievement.
Nothing can be done without hope and confidence.
~ Helen Keller

Often, one of the first signs of trouble is when a company has fewer new distributors being sponsored. Companies scramble to treat slow sponsoring as if it were a disease that can be cured with a better program, promotion or incentive. In many cases a slowdown in sponsoring is not the disease, but rather a symptom of a more serious ailment—a loss of hope. As soon as a distributor becomes convinced that the company is not the right vehicle to help them reach their goals, they stop having the ability to sponsor others with integrity. In other words, you and your team don't stop sponsoring because they don't know how or don't see the benefit, but rather because they lack the confidence they once had in the business. They lack the conviction that made it easy to invite others to do what they were doing. If you and your team don't believe the company will help you reach your long-term goals, it's incredibly difficult to convince others to join in.

Hope, or the belief that the company or its products will produce the desired result, is the life spring of direct selling. It is admittedly one of those "touchy, feely" things that no one talks about at business school, but it is so foundational to the success of your team that it requires not only consideration and conversation but it deserves your attention and a specific plan to maintain or regain it if you or your team have lost hope.

Hope is under constant attack by naysayers of the channel, and if you allow it, rumors and the thousands of lies that are carried on her wings will consume hope and leave nothing but fatigue and bitterness behind. Even in times of growth—but more deliberately in times of decline—you need to manage hope with as much attentiveness as you give to your cash.

Leaders start their teams with nothing more than a story that inspires hope and belief in their vision of what is possible, and that hope and belief is enough to hundreds and often thousands. It's not difficult for leaders to get out of practice and stop telling their hope-inspiring stories as the demands of Hyper-Growth consume them. Once your team starts to experience headwinds and slowing growth, leaders must reassume their role as "Chief

Hope Officer." They perform that duty by returning to their early days, dusting off the story of the future and broadly sharing their vision again with their leaders and their team. Leaders must be active and engaged in restoring hope and must fight to protect your team from the enemies of hope.

The H.O.P.E. Formula

Most leaders give little thought to creating hope because it is a natural by-product of "selling" others on their vision. Leaders are constantly sharing their vision and providing others evidence that their vision is possible. They share stories of product success, business success and even the success of competitors. The natural outgrowth of those activities and an output of the success of those activities is a team that has hope.

As a company matures and experiences successes and failures, leaders stop reminding their team why they should continue to be involved. By the time you recognize that your team is losing hope in their future, you need a more deliberate formula to restore hope. That formula includes:

- **H**umbly Listening to Team—having the humility to listen and be empathetic to legitimate concerns others might have without allowing your empathy to be perceived as agreement.

- **O**pen Communication—being present more often, sharing your awareness of the issues and your plans to improve them AND continuing to tell success stories. Reviving the story of why you believe in the future and reminding others of what your team has achieved so far and what it can accomplish in the future.

- **P**lan of Action—your team needs not only a business plan that can inspire hope in the future, but it also needs a plan to address any negativity that starts to consume social media conversations.

- **E**ducation—both company and field leaders need to understand that retractions are the norm. There must be a concerted effort to show all those who doubt the future the reality that other successful companies have faced similar slowing and found Renewal and significant growth on the other side.

Let's explore the H.O.P.E. formula in more detail and help you understand how to implement it in your team.

Humbly Listen to Your Team

History has shown that Hyper-Growth often breeds hubris. Founders, CEOs, top sales leaders and even corporate executives and staff often equate their success to all things positive. They begin to believe that their company has found the secret keys to success; that other companies don't have their wisdom, talent, skills, and people. Sometimes this conceit prevents the organization from perceiving the common issues that start and then accelerate a company's decline.

Earlier in my career I joined a company that had seen significant success and created dozens of financially secure field leaders. The company was justly proud of what they had accomplished and the reputation they had gained along the way. However, by the time I came onboard, sales had dropped by nearly 40% in just two years, and there was no sign of rock bottom any time soon. What surprised me most about this company was the confidence some senior field leaders had in the tactics they had unsuccessfully deployed over the previous few years.

Fortunately, I had not experienced the wild success of the past, but instead was asked to lead the Renewal of today. I started where I believe every leader should start by traveling to host listening sessions with sales leaders. They had experienced the success of the past but were also on the frontline of selling and sponsoring today. The sessions I had with dozens of leaders in each town shocked them. I had not come to teach, not come to motivate, and not come to tell. I had come to listen.

In nearly every case where I've deployed this tactic, I've found the answers... or at least identified the key issues we had to address to reach Renewal.

If you will be humble enough to start by listening, your path to Renewal will be shorter, and you will know you are addressing the right issues. You will also be preparing the ground for a renewal of hope because your team will leave those sessions convinced that you care and that you have heard them. When they know you have heard them, they will begin to believe that you will make things right again.

Hope is renewed when leaders and teams are humble enough to listen empathetically and with real intent to those they lead.

Open Communication

Open communication with your team requires leaders to walk the tightwire and find a balance between transparency and inspiration. At times I have been too transparent and left field leaders completely without hope. Conversely, without transparency it is tough to convince your team that you understand that there are problems and that you are committed to fixing them. Great communication strikes the perfect balance and leaves your team certain you understand, and confident you will fix whatever's wrong... eventually.

Sometimes challenges are compounded by the fact that there is not an effective method of communicating with your team. Excellent communication requires an actual system in place to accomplish it effectively. Your team needs to know when and how they will receive information. Field leaders typically have more than one system, but they often include weekly calls (always on the same day and at the same time), zoom meetings, monthly newsletters, weekly emails and sometimes a few texts when a message is urgent. If your team has not established predictable communications systems during your Hyper-Growth or Growth by Promotion stage, you MUST do so during the Shake-Out stage.

I learned the value of open communication with field leaders when I took over as the interim General Manager for USANA in Australia and New Zealand. When I arrived on the scene the business was in trouble in almost every imaginable way. Like many executives I've worked with, I arrived in Australia thinking that the field wouldn't know much about the state of the business. Fortunately, I set those thoughts aside and decided to begin weekly calls with all leaders who qualified at a rank equal to full-time income. During my first call I learned two things that have been universally true no matter the country, company or circumstance I've found myself in: (1) the field leaders knew exactly what was happening, way more than they should, and (2) they were grateful for my willingness to speak of the issues with openness and candor.

Each week, I invited these field leaders to join me on a conference call. I would begin each call with a "state of the company" and then I would open the call for questions. The field leader's questions, and our ensuing dialogue helped me, and my team understand what was most important to field leaders and therefore helped us prioritize tasks and improvements. These calls also gave my team a chance to hear how committed I was to make things right for the field, and that knowledge helped my team align their priorities as well.

It took us weeks to begin to make progress on the field's important issues and even longer to work through very difficult product supply and public relations issues, but that business began to grow for the first time in months within days after that first call. That is where I first gained my confidence in the power of field leaders to overcome company issues and to lead their own teams to growth.

I've seen similar results on multiple occasions in different companies. For many field leaders, the simple action of humbly listening and engaging in consistent and predictable communication is enough to restore their hope and to help them return to work with integrity.

The great truth about hope is that it doesn't require perfect plans, products or execution. It is not even a state of being but rather simply an idea planted firmly in the mind of what is likely to be. The immaterial nature of hope is both good and bad. It always favors the most credible and is often the last voice that deposits information into a willing mind. Fight to make sure your voice is the last voice and the one your team remembers and believes.

Hope always favors the most credible and is often the last voice that deposits information into a willing mind.

Plan of Action

Transparent and honest communication informed by listening with empathy and humility can make an immediate impact on hope and can even lead to hope-inspired activities that can be measured as increased sponsoring and sales. However, eventually that communication runs out of steam if there is not a sound plan and appropriate action to sustain the good feelings. After listening and understanding the critical issues faced by your team, you need not only a business plan that can inspire hope in the future, but a plan to address the negativity that often starts to consume more and more social media conversations during the Shake-Out stage.

Developing a plan to fix the issues that are holding your team back is critical and communicating that plan to the appropriate people at the appropriate time is a wise business decision. But don't forget to manage expectations and to be clear about what you *know* will work and what you *think* will work. Too often leaders secure their followers' hopes on a plan that for some reason does not work. The failure of that plan not only delays the company's return to growth, but even more tragically it destroys confidence in the leaders and makes it less likely that the next plan will restore hope or gain the support it needs to succeed.

Here are a few tactics to help you develop and execute a plan to restore hope to your team:

- *Test and Validate*
- *Have a Plan to Fight for Hope on Social Media*
- *New vs. News*

Test and Validate

When communicating your plans, make sure you leave room for testing and validation and set the expectation that changes might be required as you test the plan in the marketplace. I prefer to set expectations by assuring field leaders that "we are going to figure this out together" rather than trying to sell them on the certainty of the first plan we present. Great leaders will share their plan and their intention to validate and refine it, thereby setting the expectation that there will be a time of experimentation. In my experience, the field and employees want to know that you are committed to *a* fix, not necessarily the one and only fix you and/or your team came up with first.

Have a Plan to Fight for Hope on Social Media

In today's world, it is almost impossible to turn around sales if you don't first turn the tide on social media. Everyone is a social media reporter and unfortunately, they are able to share ideas and opinions whether or not the information has any basis in fact. Direct selling has always had its naysayers but today those who don't like the channel, those who have failed, and those who dislike another field leader, the founders or anything else have a simple way to tell the world. While most of us can easily spot those with an ax to grind, it is very difficult for people to tell what is true, what is half true and what is completely false. You owe it to your team to make sure that the information published on social media is true and that false information is refuted immediately. Even better, you should have a proactive plan to make sure there is a constant flow of good news on social media. Paying for help in producing stories and fighting the naysayers on social media is worthwhile and deserves to be part of a budget if you can find a way to afford it.

Make sure you are monitoring and responding appropriately to social media critics and that you have a plan for overwhelming your social channels with good news. Teach your leaders how and where to vent and don't allow them to use social media—ever—as their place to provide well-intended or ill-intended feedback. It may seem like a waste of time, but if you don't win online it will be tough to generate a positive return on any other investment you would prefer to make.

New vs. News

When I began my career in direct selling, the prevailing wisdom of the industry dictated that a company introduce a new product to excite their field three to four times a year. It didn't take long for companies to figure out that new product introductions were not increasing dollars per distributor/customer, but rather were just increasing costs and tying up valuable capital in inventory. More products also meant more for the field to learn. Over time, companies began to understand that there had to be a better way.

At USANA Health Sciences, we prepared for the 2002 Winter Games in Salt Lake City by using our relationship with Olympic athletes to pepper the field with news they could share; news that would make them proud to represent the company and its brand. Along the way, we learned that the field really didn't need new products as much as they just needed something new to talk about. I've become convinced that when companies don't have a plan that feeds good news to the field, the tendency is for the field to fill that communications void with rumors and worries that may or may not be true but will most assuredly destroy hope.

Having a consistent and deliberate plan to create and communicate good news often is a wise move. The more diligent you are at controlling the dialogue, the more difficult it becomes for hope-destroying rumors to find a foothold. Investing in a plan to both combat negative comments on social media and ensure that your team has a constant flow of good news to share with others is a critical and a worthwhile use of your time.

Education

Taking time to make sure your team (or at least those on your team who are building a business) understand the stages direct selling companies go through and making sure they have data to support their desire to believe the company will grow again is essential. I'm not a huge advocate of addressing a downward trajectory on the main stage at a convention or as a common theme in communication to the general field, but I do believe straight talk with meaty information is essential for top field leaders. The type of education I'm advocating can often be best presented by a third-party consultant (I have worked with ServiceQuest and WomenKind to create field presentations that can help).

These presentations should not only include information about the company or your plan, but rather facts and figures from other companies in the channel. Showing four to six company sales charts—using my business phase chart presented early in the book or one like it—and *especially* emphasizing large companies that have had growth and success after a downturn is critical. This presentation creates fertile soil to plant the seeds of hope in the form of the company's specific plans for Renewal. If you have a leader's meeting on the calendar, use it. If you don't have anything planned, it is worth the money to bring key leaders together if they have been seeing smaller paychecks month-over-month for more than six months.

As a field leader, you often recognize—before the company's leadership—when your team is starting to lose hope, and you can begin to restore it using the H.O.P.E. formula. Remember that most of the time, there are teams that are able to insulate themselves during a corporate-wide downturn and continue to experience growth in sales, commissions, and advancements. Great field leaders will implement the H.O.P.E. formula and help their team get back on track sooner.

As the leader of a team, you are the primary keeper of hope. Your role cannot be delegated to downline leaders or the company's executives or founders. Your team's attitude, belief and vision for the future is your responsibility. If you want to meet your long-term goals, you must fight for hope at all costs. Great leaders are able to help their team weather difficult periods in the company's history and often will have organizations that are immune to the downturn others are experiencing. Over my many years of observing successful teams in action, I've seen great leaders deploy the following tactics to preserve or renew hope:

- *They Have Rules for Team Groups on Social Media*
- *They Are Part of the Solution*
- *They Set and Sustain a Positive Tone*
- *They Don't Try to Become Customer Service*
- *They Take Care of Themselves*

They Have Rules for Team Groups on Social Media

Great leaders use social media to communicate and train their team and they also set ground rules for being part of those groups from day one. They teach their team and 1:1 they teach each leader how and where to vent, making it clear that their social media group is not a place to share negative content.

Leaders delete any thread that is designed or has the potential to destroy confidence and hope, and they communicate verbally (by phone or in person) to the offending team member in the spirit of teaching. The first time someone goes negative they earn 1:1 instruction. The second time they are removed from the group.

They Are Part of the Solution

I recently met with a CEO who had seen his large company decline significantly in the past year. We had met early in that decline and I had encouraged him to refocus the company on a simple system of acquiring customers that would be an evolution of the Facebook focus that had brought their initial growth. On this specific occasion the CEO enthusiastically told me of a meeting he'd had with a top leader task force. During that meeting, a leader had asked permission to share with the group some of the success she was having on her team. Given her helpful (versus accusatory) tone, she was allowed to present. The CEO described how this leader had come with a thoughtful presentation that showed what was working, why it was working and how it could scale. She then clearly outlined the changes to current programs and technology that would be required to implement this proven program across the company.

The company is in the process of testing this program as I write this. The CEO expressed to me how grateful he was for a leader who went beyond criticism to actually think through a solution that she had tested with her team. My career has taught me that most (maybe 90%) of the best ideas come from the field, but most field ideas (maybe 90%) aren't scalable or can't be implemented as they are first presented. Your company needs your ideas, but even more importantly they need you to test and experiment with your own team so that you can refine and help make the idea work for others.

Don't make your ideas a "do or die" issue for you. Be productive and helpful, but if the company doesn't adopt your concept, be open and teachable to other alternatives. Don't take it personally. The goal is not for you to win an argument but rather to make sure the company finds a way to grow again so that you, your team and everyone else can win.

Set and Sustain a Positive Tone

Great leaders reach out to other crossline leaders and lock arms with them in a commitment to not allow anyone with a negative attitude to hijack their company. Leaders have issues and need someone to talk with, so they create a safe and private place to have those discussions and they always leave with their own hope intact. Just like the water in a river always flows to the lowest point downstream, organizations (of all types) will descend into negativity if allowed to run without proactive leadership. Fighting the natural tendency of your team to turn negative will be a fight that will require significant mental energy. Find confidantes and partners to fight alongside you. Don't try and go it alone and do hold each other accountable to a high standard of positive leadership. If you lack unity with other crossline leaders, consider working with an outside facilitator who is skilled at working with direct selling leaders. I highly recommend Milan Jensen of Womenkind (www.womenkind.com) who has worked miracles with crossline leaders and has decades of personal experience as both a direct selling executive and the leader of a large field team.

Milan told me that she learned early in her tenure as a leader how important it was to avoid being drawn into a negative conversation. Milan said, "relationships in the field grow with time, and are often very closely tied to friends and family. When a leader is confronted with someone in their team who is confiding their lack of trust or hope, the leader must listen well and avoid the tendency to feel responsible or obligated to agree, even if you do. Remember, your team member does not really want you to agree. They want to be heard and they want hope from their leader."

Don't Try to Become Customer Service

In every company I've worked with, we have been able to find plenty of positive, capable people to work for an hourly wage (just above minimum wage) to answer the phone and provide customer service. Unfortunately, it is like finding a needle in a haystack to acquire someone who can build, train, and motivate a large team of direct sellers. So, I find it terribly tragic when the few who are capable leaders decide to express their natural urge to serve others by committing to provide personal customer service to their customers or their team. No matter how bad you think your customer service is, you cannot turn in your mantle of leadership for a customer service headset. When the going gets tough, your team needs your leadership. You won't have the time or mental energy to provide that guidance and support if you are the chief customer service officer on your team. Please resist the natural urge to try and fix things that customer service can and should fix.

They Take Care of Themselves

Leaders like to solve problems so often the needs of the team will take a priority over personal well-being. Revisit your daily personal practice of selfcare. Find a way to take a break from the demands of your business. Do something that will help you sustain a positive perspective—so that you are better equipped to lead. Milan Jensen warned, "You simply can't function well from an empty cup, and your cup will drain quickly in times of renewal."

Take care of yourself so that you have enough emotional energy to take care of others. Only you will know what you need, but whatever your prescription to feel well and to remain happy may be—fill it.

Chapter 7: Innovation—*A Field Leader's Guide*

Learning and innovation go hand in hand. The
arrogance of success is to think that what you did
yesterday will be sufficient for tomorrow.
~ William Pollard, Physicist & Priest

My greatest worry in writing this book is that readers will see the word "innovation" and skip the following chapters believing they already understand the content. These readers assume I mean "new products" and may be surprised to hear that I believe new products have as good a chance of leading to further decline than to renewed growth.

While most focus their innovation on new products, I hope you will agree that Renewal can more often be found by considering innovations in:

- The compensation and rewards systems,
- The methods (or system) your team uses to acquire new customers, and/or
- The introduction of new technology or tech enabled tools.

We will discuss selling systems, product innovation and compensation and rewards innovation, but first let me introduce the concept of innovation boundaries.

Boundaries Governing Innovation

In the chart below, I've attempted to provide a simple visual to help you understand that there are boundaries within which a company has permission to introduce (and is likely to find success with) new products. Too often, companies that have actually established meaning in their brands in a specific product category—Longaberger in the basket market, for example—will try and redefine their brand as a distribution brand (like Amway, Walmart, Target, etc.) and give itself permission to introduce a wide variety of products. While redefining a brand is possible, especially if you use visual renewal to reset consumer thinking, companies often then run into trouble trying to sell unrelated products because their field has a system for selling Product A and not one for selling Product B.

For example, while Amway established its brand as a distributor of multiple brands of products and thereby gave itself permission to introduce almost every product category, their field had not learned how to sell real estate and the system required to sell real estate would have forced the company to introduce an entirely new selling system—not just a new product.

As the visual below depicts, the ideal new products will fit between the existing boundaries set by our brand and the selling systems distributors have been successfully using in the past.

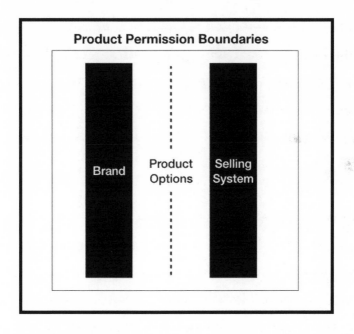

Brand Boundaries

Most of us understand that brands have meaning. That meaning can grant a company permission to introduce certain products or it may restrict the company from introducing others. For example, Microsoft started as a software operating system but has successfully expanded its brand's meaning so that customers have given the company permission to introduce productivity software (MS Word, PowerPoint, etc.) and eventually computer hardware like the Microsoft Surface. However, if Microsoft tried to introduce a line of football helmets, few athletes would trust the protection of their head to a company with no related experience. While it is possible to extend the expertise of your brand and gain customer permission to produce new products that are related to your core, introducing products that have no clear relationship to your brand only weakens your brand and makes the product a "generic."

Systems and System Innovation

When I talk about "systems" I'm talking about a recorded way of accomplishing something that eliminates the need for someone to figure out how to do "it" themselves. Author and educator Eric Worre said that you know you have a great system when "everyone knows it, everyone does it, and it works."

I discovered systems accidentally as we grew Team Beachbody from $35 million to $380 million in just three years. Eric Worre, however, helped me by articulating with clarity six specific systems to which I have added two more to make it an even eight. In my opinion, the key to exponential growth is for a company (most often through its sales leaders) to have a few of these eight systems in place:

Direct Selling's Eight Systems:

1. **Customer Acquisition**—a simple and repeatable way to start a discussion with a prospect and to convince them to make their first purchase.

2. **Distributor Upgrade/Acquisition**—a simple and repeatable way to approach your most enthusiastic customers and convert them to becoming a seller.

3. **New Distributor Training System**—a simple and repeatable way to help a new seller achieve success and confidence.

4. **Distributor Advancement System**—a simple and repeatable way of helping new distributors advance to a place of profitability within the compensation system.

5. **Recognition System**—I owe this insight to Milan Jensen who reminded me that leaders need a system in place that defines when and how they will recognize the achievements of their team members.

6. **Convention Attendance System**—this is all Eric Worre and not something I had discovered on my own, but after listening to him I'm convinced that companies need a system in place to get serious distributors to their annual convention.

7. **Communications System**—a simple and repeatable way to provide ongoing information and training to distributors.

8. **Leadership Development & Training**—a simple and repeatable way to help field leaders acquire the business and management skills necessary to lead a large organization and effectively influence their team.

While I've come to believe there is great value in understanding and methodically implementing all of these systems, it is my experience that growth and Renewal can take place by effectively focusing on the first one: customer acquisition. I also believe that this work is best done by field leaders and then expanded (if desired) beyond the leader's team with help from the corporate executive team.

As we talk about innovation, I will particularly focus on the opportunity to innovate and renew the customer acquisition system and even more importantly the critical requirement that new product innovation be restricted to the company's customer acquisition system. Let me explain.

If You've Grown, You Have a Customer Acquisition System

In a phone call with the CEO of a struggling direct selling company, I asked her what the company's customer acquisition system was during peak growth.

"That's the problem," she said. "We don't have a system and never have had a system!"

I knew this company had experienced significant growth and I now know that growth doesn't happen without a system, but the above conversation wasn't the time or place to convince this CEO of that fact. However, I do hope to convince you today.

Every successful direct selling company has a customer acquisition system, but like my CEO friend, surprisingly few executives understand what their system is. That is a bold claim, but years of experience have confirmed it in company after company. How can a company have success and not understand the system that is generating their sales? Often the system driving sales is discovered by you, the field leaders. Your experience of trial and error and try again, along with your everyday connection with customers, provides you the perfect opportunity to create, refine and perfect a system of sales. Shockingly few companies have taken the time to learn exactly what field leaders are using to generate sales. For many (perhaps most) the independent field leaders define the system and teach their teams with little or no support from the company. That is why I believe this is one of the best uses of your time during Renewal.

One company that didn't initially understand the customer acquisition system developed in the field is Herbalife at the beginning of one of their multiple waves of success. One of the company's waves of success in the United States came as a result of a program developed in Mexico. Rather than attempting to sell a monthly supply of their leading product, Formula 1®, Herbalife's distributors in Mexico offered single servings from their home or workplace and called them "Nutrition Clubs." At first, Herbalife's executives reportedly didn't understand the program and even tried to prevent it from being taught in the U.S. despite the fact that it worked in the Latino communities. Fortunately for Herbalife, they were not successful in stopping this practice and eventually were forced to accept it. Herbalife's impressive growth in the U.S. Latino community started as a result of this distributor-led customer acquisition system that was imported from Mexico by field leaders, and then eventually embraced and supported by the corporate team at Herbalife.

In the spring of 2017, Nu Skin had a sudden and unexpected revival of sales in the United States. Despite the company's impressive investment in research and development and significant corporate efforts to increase sales, the new sales surge came from an almost forgotten product Nu Skin had been selling for more than ten years. Why? Led by the success of a new distributor in the United Kingdom and follow-on success by a new distributor in the U.S., Nu Skin's field leaders learned how to use social media to share before and after pictures of their decade-old AP 24® Whitening Fluoride Toothpaste to drive demand and increase sales.

Nu Skin executives were wise enough to set aside other initiatives and align behind the momentum of both the product and the social sharing method of selling. Newly appointed Nu Skin CEO Ritch Wood had a sexy, tech-focused strategy to talk about as he took over and the company has followed its field to deploy tech tools designed to support the simple system. As is so often the case, Nu Skin's selling system was accidentally discovered by distributors with a combined tenure of fewer than six months with the company. To the credit of Nu Skin's management team, they were astute enough to recognize and capitalize on the system and reap its benefits.

Innovating the Customer Acquisition System

Often a company can experience slowed growth and declining field participation because they have failed to innovate and help the field discover a new customer acquisition system. Perfectly good systems can become outdated and need to be replaced for two reasons:

- **Field Fatigue**
- **Social Media/Technology Changes**

Field Fatigue

Unlike a manufacturing system that can be deployed and kept in place for decades with only the need for maintenance from time to time, the systems used in direct selling depend on human beings who get fatigued even if the system is working. During my tenure at Beachbody, weight loss "challenges" became popular and Beachbody, AdvoCare, ViSalus and others built very successful customer acquisition systems around them and grew by hundreds of millions of dollars. By the time I joined AdvoCare, "challenges" still worked, but the field leaders were tired of deploying them and were in desperate need of a new system. In other words, there was still confidence in the products, but the field was tired of doing the same thing year after year and the customer acquisition system was in need of an update. As we began to bring freshness to the customer acquisition system, we began to see renewed energy and participation in the field.

Social Media/Technology Changes

As Facebook moved off of college campuses to become a main street social connection tool, several direct selling companies learned how to do business very effectively on the platform. Younique, Jamberry, Beachbody, and many others saw rapid growth as their field leaders acquired customers on Facebook. While Facebook is still the largest social media platform in terms of total usage, the growth of users and commerce has been migrating to Instagram and YouTube, and few direct sellers have figured out how to adapt or augment their customer acquisitions to these new platforms. Clearly, one of the biggest innovation opportunities awaiting direct sellers is to help distributors identify a system for acquiring customers on new social platforms.

Where to Find Systems

Creating customer acquisition systems (or any of the identified systems) is most often a process of discovery rather than of creation. For companies that have sales and thousands of sellers, the process of identifying a new customer acquisition system that can serve as a catalyst for renewed growth begins by identifying those individuals and teams who are growing.

During my tenure at Beachbody, I recognized early on that the company's early growth had not come from traditional recruiting and selling activities but from the identification of founding leaders who brought with them some experienced direct sellers who were close to them. The rest of the growth came as a result of leads the company curated for its distributors from its television direct marketing campaigns. Beachbody sold its fitness programs via infomercial and then assigned all of the customers who were upsold nutritionals by their tele-sales department to their "distributors." In my interviews with top leaders I heard stories of receiving checks without knowing how they were earned. When the company discontinued the aggressive lead program, sales in Team Beachbody (their direct sales division) plummeted from a $50 mm+ run rate to a $36 mm run rate.

After traveling to meet with most of the company's top leaders, I began to study the financial results and noticed that many of the top sellers were using social media despite our sales team's strong opposition to that practice. I reached out to those top sellers and told them of my interest in learning from them and invited them to the office for a few days of dialogue. I invited each of these sellers to stand and share with the others what they were doing and what they had learned and allowed the others to ask questions. I sat in the back of the room feverishly taking notes and chimed in with my own questions from time to time. Some of the sellers were more open than others. Most came with concern that the company had called them in to punish them. All left that event having created new allies and having learned from each other. I left the gathering knowing that I had to:

- **Choose a System That Could Be Duplicated and Scaled**
- **Develop a Method of Testing and Refining the System**
  - **Figure Out How to Align Your Team Around the New System**

Below I will share what I've learned and my advice for identifying new systems to support and scale your team.

Choosing System That Can Be Duplicated and Scaled

As you begin to study the individuals and smaller teams in your organization who are having success, it will become clear which ones understand and use systems and which ones are just extraordinary salespersons.

Throughout my career I had heard over and over again how important people were to success in business. Expert after expert taught that the most successful companies are those that find and enable the best people. Then I read Michael Gerber's account of the founding of McDonald's in his book *The E-Myth Revisited* and my paradigm for direct selling changed forever. Gerber wrote that McDonald's founders Richard and Maurice McDonald realized that they could not attract excellent workers to help them in their restaurant and therefore redesigned their operations to allow below-average employees to produce consistently high-quality products. Ray Kroc eventually discovered the brilliance of that philosophy and the rest is history.

Too many direct selling companies focus on great products, excellent compensation systems and eye-popping marketing and neglect the difficult work of making their customer acquisition system something that is simple enough to ensure the success of below-average distributors. Don't take your eye off my point by assuming I'm encouraging you to ignore great people or to not even aspire to have great people on your team. That is not the point. The point is that you need systems that great people can blow up, but that below-average people can also use to achieve their goals and dreams.

As you study the success of those who are growing their business, your primary objective is to separate success that is the result of a great or extraordinary person from success that is a result of an extraordinary and simple system. You are looking for systems, not people, because you can plug anyone into a great system, and they will succeed. You can scale with systems faster than you can scale with people.

> *You can plug anyone into a great system, and they will succeed. Therefore, you can scale with great systems faster than you can scale with great people.*

It is possible that there are no effective systems, and, in that case, you will be forced to create your own. You should be able to find best practices from multiple people and piece them together into a system. If that is the case for you, I would start by asking—and using experimentation and actual human-to-human experience—to answer the following questions:

- How does one start a discussion about our products with a potential customer? What are the exact words that come out of the seller's mouth? Are they starting from scratch or putting themselves in front of someone who is already looking for your solution? Systems that fail to give sellers the words to use to start a dialogue only work with great conversationalists and fail the "below-average person" test.

- How does one prepare someone to receive an invitation to purchase or try your product? What are the words of the invitation? How do you bundle the invitation with an offer so compelling that the invitation is more likely to be acted upon?

Here are a few examples of the most effective customer acquisition systems:

- **Arbonne International's "Try this" System**—Arbonne's sellers were taught to drop off their entire line of skincare products with a prospect and say, "I think you are going to love what this skincare does for you and I'm so confident I'm going to let you try the entire line for one week. After a week, I'm going to come by and if you love it, I'll pick up a check. If you don't love it, I'll pick up the product."

- **Beachbody, AdvoCare, ViSalus's "Weight Loss Challenge"**—"If you're ready to lose weight, come join our accountability group. We are going to help each other earn the prizes our company is offering as part of its challenge."

- **Younique's "Social Video Demonstrations"**— "Don't take my word for it, look at all the customers who are having noticeable results from our product."

- **Beachbody**'s **"See for Yourself Results"**— "Look at all of the people who are losing weight as a result of my coaching. If you want to lose weight, come join my team and I'll get you started with the most compelling starter pack!"

- **Nu Skin's "Before and After Teeth Whitening"**—"Here are my before and after pictures. After using this toothpaste for X days, my teeth are whiter. If you want whiter teeth, DM me."

- **AdvoCare's "Spark Me!"**— "If you are feeling tired every day and don't seem to have the energy to make it through your afternoon, call me and I'll give you a FREE three-day sample of Spark. Don't take my word for it, try it and see for yourself."

- **Monat Global's "Meet Monat"**— "Join us for a meet-up at (wine bar, bistro). If you have been looking for a great hair care line or a network marketing opportunity, then join me!"

As you can see, great systems are bold and simple. The easiest to duplicate focus on a specific verifiable product benefit. Notice that I'm focused on customer acquisition systems here. Although there are examples of companies that grew primarily with a distributor acquisition system, I believe those days are behind us. While a company needs a great opportunity, the most successful are leading with customer acquisition and then have in place a system for identifying and upgrading their most fanatical customers.

Develop a Method of Testing and Refining the System

Unless you have found a group on your team with recent success with systems similar to the one you are advocating, most of your team members are understandably skeptical of any selling systems that come from the company. I am among the corporate executives who have been guilty of being arrogant enough to believe I could create and teach field leaders "how to sell" even though I had never sold anything myself. My experience has taught me that when it comes to creating new sales systems, there is no substitute for testing and validation.

Once you have found, refined or created a customer acquisition system to accompany your current product line or a new product line you plan to introduce, you need to find a way to validate that your system works in practice. It is very challenging to test a new system if it is being designed for a new product that you don't want to preannounce. Your only option is to find employees or hire previous sellers as consultants to test your theory in real world focus groups. Early in my career, I worked with a large consumer packaged goods company that was experimenting with the idea of selling a new home-delivery food line via direct selling. In this case, we hired a former direct seller and used family and friends of corporate executives to test our theories in several markets. While these tests aren't 100% reliable, they are directionally helpful.

Most of the time you will be working on updating or introducing a customer acquisition system designed to work with existing products. I believe the best way to validate these systems is to work with leaders who don't have a strong commitment to their own system, are loyal to the company, are willing to trial the system as system they didn't design. Ideally you want team members to help you test your new system who:

- **Are respected by others**—they can help you sell the system to others if it works.
- **Are actively working**—you want those who will deploy your system often, not just once or twice.
- **Are collaborative by nature**—you want team members who will deploy your system as it was

designed (not as they think it should be designed) and then work to improve it from there.

- **Can be trusted to keep secrets**—eventually you will want the world to know about systems that work, but you don't want someone who will erode confidence by sharing the inevitable failures you may experience during your testing.

Align Your Team Around Your New System

Once you have validated the effectiveness of your new system you will want to introduce it and convince the majority of your team to migrate from the systems they are using to yours. In my experience, it is not reasonable to believe that ALL will migrate and support the new system. I also do not advocate forcing or coercing them to do so. Instead I've found that the best systems eventually sell themselves. Therefore, my approach to implementing new systems is to delay a large reveal and instead slowly expand your test... first as a beta limited to only those who will deploy it by giving it their full support. The ideal introduction will take time and will be more of a "pull" than a "push" strategy. As leaders in your beta begin to have success and talk about it, others who are struggling will want to learn how they can deploy the system on their team. Ideally, the system will be old news and your team will be begging for it by the time it is officially introduced.

Have you heard the saying "go slow to go fast"? In my opinion the fastest way to gain adoption is to introduce it slowly and only as others are demanding it.

During the period of alignment, you will have team members who will criticize the system or argue that there doesn't need to be a single way of acquiring customers. This is true, and I believe you can and should verbally support systems taught by successful team members. But you should focus your time and attention on supporting the system you have introduced if it is delivering results.

As we committed to the Challenge system at Beachbody, it was a great system because everybody knew it, everybody did it, and it worked. This new system became an engine of renewed growth because it required almost no training. Coaches had a "copy and paste" system to follow to achieve sales.

With the customer acquisition system in place, we were able to create a simple coach recruiting system (or Customer to Coach Upgrade System). Recruiting new Coaches became simple. Coaches were taught to listen for customers who talked about being asked if they'd lost weight and were given language to turn those conversations into recruiting opportunities with the simple question, "Have you ever thought of doing what I do?"

Our on-boarding system was simple to create because most of our new Coaches had been part of a Challenge Group and therefore, they knew exactly what we wanted new Coaches to do.

Aligning around a customer acquisition system is not simple. It takes hard work and I don't think it can be done in less than 18 months, but your team can experience growth as the system is perfected and introduced. Whatever the cost in trial, error and patience, the end result is so powerful for a team and can help your entire company. I believe there is no better way for a leader to spend its time during a period of Renewal than to focus on system innovation. With the exception of a historically few unicorn new products, in my opinion there is no innovation that can improve results faster than to align around a powerful customer acquisition system.

Common Mistakes Leaders Make

While field leaders more often than not are the source of system innovation, many make mistakes in working with their team and/or with the company executive team. Let me point out a few common mistakes field leaders make when it comes to systems:

- ***Waiting for Corporate***—If your corporate team doesn't have a system, isn't working on one, or has one that is out of touch with reality, you are in the majority. Don't wait for your company to figure things out. Push forward and begin experimenting with systems until you find those that work for your team. Realize that you will have to be thoughtful about who on your team is invited to help with your experiment and you'll have to communicate clearly with those participating so they understand your goal is to pilot something you can introduce to others and is NOT to subvert the company's system.

- ***You're Not a Good Proxy for What Works*—** Notice I said to experiment until you find a system that works for your *team* and not for *you*. If you are a field leader, chances are you are extraordinary and therefore what works for you probably won't work for most of your team. Remember that your goal is to empower the least skilled member of your team. Great systems make below-average people successful.

- ***Allowing the Best to Be Enemy of "Good Enough"*—**Some day you may evolve and have the best system, but your team needs systems that are good enough first because chances are they will do nothing (or very little) unless you give them something that shows them what to do.

- ***Keeping Your System or the Process "Confidential"***—When developing systems, you want as many good people involved as possible. Just because someone is crossline doesn't mean they shouldn't be involved. Find crossline leaders to work with. Split the load and have one person focus on one system (customer acquisition) while the other focuses on another (upgrading customers to distributors). The power of systems is truly experienced when "everyone is doing it" and the company doesn't have to choose an organization to support.

How Field Leaders Should Support Product Innovation

While new products play a very important role in jump starting or continuing the growth of direct selling companies, not all new products play an equally important role. Some selling systems are more dependent on new products than others. Understanding the role of new products and being clear about the type of new product being introduced will help you and your team make the most of any new product introduction.

New Products Must Fit the Customer Acquisition System

New products are often thought of as the key driver to increase growth. However, a few direct selling companies understand the customer acquisition system being used by their distributors and make sure new products don't disrupt that system. These few companies work with field leaders to ensure that the products are introduced with an accompanying sales system. Or, they deliberately teach distributors to continue to focus on the "lead story" and how to use the new product as a follow-on opportunity for existing customers or for prospects that don't respond to the lead. But there are plenty of companies who don't understand selling systems, and therefore you as a field leader need to make sure you understand how to respond to all types of new product innovation.

For example, catalog companies like Avon, Home Interiors, Pampered Chef and Thirty-One Gifts rely on innovative and seasonal products to give customers a reason to return to a party or to look through their most recent catalog. Executives from these companies will argue that managing their product pipeline is one of their most important responsibilities. On the other hand, most network marketing companies rely on a hero product and it's likely their customer acquisition system is built around that single product. Companies with hero products or with product packs focused on a single benefit (e.g. weight loss) struggle to effectively use new products.

I learned this lesson early in my career at USANA Health Sciences where we had a sales force that was leading with our core vitamin and mineral product, the Essentials. Our founder was a scientist and the story told by our distributors all led to the Essentials. However, a majority of the management team became convinced that we needed a skincare line, so we launched a very good line with a tie-in to the company's science-based founding. The line initially sold out as current distributors and customers ordered the product to sample it for themselves and their families. To make sure we could keep up with demand we acquired a manufacturer to make the product for us. In the end, it never grew beyond the current base and never became a significant seller. In fact, the entire line made up less than 10% of sales and the field struggled to find any new customers for any of our products until they decided to ignore the new skin care line and go back to telling the story they knew about the Essentials. As a field leader, you need to know when you should ignore new products (or at least not attempt to use them to acquire new customers).

A similar thing happened to AdvoCare just before I joined the company. They introduced a "Fit" line with great data to support that the "Weekend Warrior" target market was robust and growing. Unfortunately, AdvoCare's salesforce had effectively grown using a customer acquisition system focused on weight loss. They knew how to use weight loss products to acquire new customers and didn't have a system to acquire Weekend Warriors even though there were plenty of them in the field. With no system in place to sell this new line, the distributors purchased it for their own use, recommended it from time to time, and continued to struggle. Within weeks of joining the company, we refocused our time and attention on weight loss, renewed our weight loss-based customer acquisition system and began to see our topline slowly but surely improve for the first time in three years.

These two companies are not alone. Younique tried to build on the launch of a fragrance line despite the fact that their presenters ("presenters" being the title Younique uses for its distributors) knew how to use mascara to acquire new customers. Longaberger tried to launch jewelry despite the fact that their distributors knew how to sell home décor and specifically, baskets. Company after company pulls out their product innovation playbook and launches what they believe will be a transformational new product line only to disappoint their field and their factories.

Product innovation without proper consideration for the customer acquisition needed to sell a new product is a recipe for failure... not only failure to meet expectations but also continued failure to renew growth

The ideal is for companies to work hand-in-hand with their field leaders to create a unified marketing and sharing system that makes it easy for the field and leaves new reps thinking, "I can do that" and leaves company management crystal clear in their understanding of how to deploy company resources to support that system. However, far too many companies leave the selling system to their independent distributors, so as a leader it is critical that you take the time to decide how to create a new system for products that are truly transformational or to teach your team how to remain focused on your hero while using new products and recommending them to existing customers.

Is Your New Product Revolutionary or Evolutionary?

For the most part, I know most field leaders want to avoid disappointing corporate executives. If the company sets an expectation for a product, leaders want to meet that expectation. However, often companies will launch what is essentially a good product line extension—an evolutionary product—in a way that makes the field believe the product is a unicorn that deserves all of your time and attention now... a revolutionary product.

As the leader of a team, you need to determine if a new product is revolutionary or evolutionary. Evolutionary products should be launched with clear instruction to your team on how it complements the current customer acquisition system, which should be built around a hero product. In other words, make sure your team doesn't lead with the evolutionary new product, but instead uses it to try and generate additional sales from current customers while they continue to acquire new ones with the hero product.

If a product has the potential of becoming a new hero, I would focus your time on working on the system for selling it. I would only focus my team on a second hero if I was confident my first hero had outlived its useful life. Having two heroes at the same time is like having two quarterbacks. It is not impossible, but there is not a lot of data to show that it can work as effectively as focusing does.

A Few Last Thoughts on Product Innovation

What should you do when a blockbuster product sells out? There are several amazing examples of how sudden demand for existing products or response to new products has completely changed the trajectory of direct selling companies. For example:

- ***SeneGence***—had a distributor figure out how to demonstrate the durability of their lipstick and a company with steady sales experienced Hyper-Growth overnight.

- ***Nu Skin***—a new distributor figured out how to use before and after pictures to sell their ten-year-old whitening toothpaste. The product flew off the shelves and the company experienced renewed growth in North America.

- **LuLaRoe**—figured out how to sell stretchy pants with unique patterns and couldn't keep them in stock.
- **Younique**—launched 3D and years later 4D mascara and sold out on multiple occasions despite "aggressive" forecasting.
- **Origami Owl**—had to use a waiting list to accommodate demand from new distributors when the story of Bella Weems' new locket jewelry went viral.

If you are fortunate to find a product that you can't keep in stock, don't despair. I know being out of stock is especially hard and embarrassing for you and your team, but don't allow your team to focus on the negative and miss the chance to benefit from the upside of being "sold out." Rejoice in your good fortune, communicate clearly with your team and make sure to tell the world. There is nothing like true, unplanned scarcity to drive growth and companies that do their best to meet demand and spend time adjusting their core customer acquisition system around their new blockbuster product usually win. Be careful not to assume you have your new customer acquisition system just because you have more customers than you need. Scarcity is a great growth driver, but its utility is, well... scarce. When the scarcity is gone, if your team has only learned how to use scarcity to attract others, your growth will dry up immediately. Great products can grow sales, but only when coupled with a great system can it sustain them.

Technology Innovation

Many leaders will be tempted to push their company to deploy new technology tools and some leaders will contract to offer products to their team. I would guard against being one of them unless you have a very mature team with mature systems, and you know exactly how the new technology will support your system.

Often, companies and leaders acquire new technologies that don't fit their method of doing business and they are forced to adopt a less effective way of doing business to accommodate the technology they acquire.

There are a few direct selling companies that define themselves from day one as "technology companies." They have committed to a path that will require them to continue to make technology innovation a central part of their strategy going forward. For the vast majority of direct sellers, technology innovation typically follows system and product innovation, but it doesn't lead. I believe technology is important, but rarely should direct selling companies rely on technology innovation to renew their growth. I often hear of companies that want to invest significant dollars in technology before they really understand the customer acquisition system. In my opinion, those companies lock themselves into "systems" that utilize the technology effectively, but don't necessarily drive new growth and sales. Therefore, my advice to most companies is to save their money and avoid developing or acquiring new technology tools until they are clear about the systems they will rely on to grow. Once they know their systems, deciding on what technology they need will be simple and the tools developed or acquired will likely be used.

Field Leader Dos and Don'ts

Field leaders need to have their own clarity around how new products fit into their team's selling system. Leaders need to recognize when a product is *evolutionary* and should be sold to existing customers as follow-on purchase options and when a product is *revolutionary* and needs its own customer acquisition system. This decision is critical and requires decisiveness because a team with two customer acquisition systems is no better off than a team with none. Here are my suggestions for field leaders:

- ***Don't Let Your Team Get Distracted by a New Product or Product Line***—If your team is selling weight loss and you're given a weight training product, don't let your team stop selling weight loss to start selling this new product. Teach them how to offer it to existing customers (hopefully, you have a system for that) and then refocus your team on the customer acquisition system that is working.

- ***Recognize Revolutionary Products and Pivot***— If your company does come out with a new product that is much better or easier to sell than others, take the time to create a customer acquisition system to sell the new product and teach your team to pivot to the new system (not to add the new system). Great growth comes when teams have a single customer acquisition system and, if necessary, a system for upselling other products to existing customers.

- ***Create a System for Selling Non-Hero Products***—Hero products are those that you build your customer acquisition system around. It can be one product or a product bundle, but it's not "all products." If your team has learned to acquire customers with a hero product and your company continues to introduce more and more products, you need a system for selling these new products to existing customers, so your team doesn't try and use these new products to acquire new customers. I've seen far too many distributors stop growing because they were trying to sell non-hero products to new customers. Field leaders owe it to their team to make it super clear which product(s) they acquire customers with and which products they sell to existing customers.

Chapter 8: Simplify—*Removing Layers to Discover the Core*

The art of simplicity is a puzzle of complexity.
~ Douglas Horton, Dean, Harvard Divinity School

When I think of simplicity I think of Apple and its founder Steve Jobs, who said, "That's been one of my mantras—focus and simplicity. Simple can be harder than complex: you have to work hard to get your thinking clean to make it simple. But it's worth it in the end because once you get there, you can move mountains."

What Simplifying is NOT

For most, getting to simple will include answering the question "What should we stop doing?" But that's not all. Mostly it is about making things more predictable for your organization. In other words, simplicity is less about doing fewer things and more about having fewer surprises.

> ***Simplicity is less about doing fewer things
> and more about having fewer surprises.***

I love to use the analogy of Christmas when I talk about simplicity. Most of us don't want fewer presents at Christmas, and most of us want to be surprised Christmas morning, but none of us wants to wake up and suddenly learn that today is Christmas. Surprises are only manageable when those who must act to create the response aren't surprised by the timing or expectation. Companies that randomly surprise field leaders and then expect them to execute and mobilize their teams will eventually wear out their field—even though they are "giving" them great new products that should help them make money. Instead of springing new programs on your team, create a calendar and provide your leaders clear expectations and tools to execute with so they are prepared to partner with you and magnify the results with their teams

Simplicity is sometimes not about doing less, but rather about surprising people less.

Simplifying the Complexity of Simplifying

As Steve Jobs said in the quote cited earlier, the work of making things simple is so, so difficult and requires WAY more finesse than making things good enough. Getting to the point where your team recognizes and acknowledges that you have simplified things for them will take time but let me give you a framework that will help you jump-start the process. I call it the **Three C's of Simplification:**

- *Calendar*—start with a calendar with a full year published in advance.
- *Cadence*—think carefully about how often your team needs something (promotion, incentive, meetings), how often the company is providing something (convention, new products, etc.), and create a consistent cadence. Good organizations have a rhythm their team can clap along with.
- *Communication*—teams that are simple to work with have a consistent communication system and everyone knows when, how, and from whom they can expect to hear about specific topics.

Calendar—Publish Your Plan for a Full Year

For the first decade of my career in direct selling this headline would have been like the fast forward button I would have pressed to skip to the next point as soon as possible. Like many of you, it seemed like I was always operating in response mode. If that sounds like you and your team, the thought of publishing a calendar a year in advance seems impossible, but it's not. You simply start with what you know and improve your calendar over time.

I learned the power of a calendar from an architect, a soft-spoken, humble man by the name of Bill Nelson who volunteered as my advisor in a church assignment I had in my mid-thirties. I was responsible for overseeing a home-to-home ministering program that paired two members of our church and assigned them to visit and "watch over" a few families. My role was to visit with each of these companionships every quarter to see how their families where doing and to find out if there was anything the church could do to help them. I loved the concept and I had every intent of fulfilling my commitment, but I was a busy executive and traveling all the time. The quarters would fly by before I would get around to meeting with anyone.

Bill was supportive and recognized my desire to serve. He asked if he could make a suggestion and I said "Sure!"

"Why don't you take time now to schedule your four interviews with each companionship for the entire year," he said. "You might end up traveling or they might have something come up, but it will be much easier for you to reschedule than to be constantly scheduling."

I took Bill's advice. It worked like a charm.

I've applied Bill's tactic as an executive in every company I've worked in since that conversation. I know what I want to do (be in the field two to four days every month), which conferences I want to attend, what direct reports I should meet with and how often I want to talk with them, and what "big events" I have at home (anniversary, first day of school, etc.). At the beginning of each year, I put those on my calendar and fill in new details that come along or make revisions as necessary.

You will be surprised at how much you know if you will just sit down, answer the following questions and begin making notations in your calendar:

- When is our annual convention?
- What other field meetings/visits should I schedule (or how often)? Publishing a calendar that simply says "leader meetings" in May can be sufficient as a starting point.
- What promotions do we want to support or start this year? (e.g. Black Friday, Back-to-School, Valentine's, Mother's Day, etc.)
- When will we communicate (conference calls, emails, newsletters, etc.)?
- When will we introduce or go on our annual incentive trip? (Hint: don't put the location on

the calendar if it hasn't been announced. Just say "annual incentive trip.")

Providing your team with a calendar that helps them anticipate and plan for announcements and "surprises" will immediately make things feel more straightforward and will increase morale and excitement. One other advantage: the calendar will also communicate sustainability. As many of you have learned, whenever sales start to decline, people immediately begin to fear the worst— "We are going out of business!" Publishing a calendar is a subtle way of anchoring your team in the future again and helping to offset that negative thinking.

Cadence

I may be the worst dancing partner on the planet, and I hung up my baritone after the 8th grade. No one has accused me of being a musician since. But I know enough about dancing and music to understand that great songs are built on a foundation of a clearly defined rhythm. The most excellent dancers, composers and musicians are inspired by the rhythm established at the beginning of a score and often kept by a skilled percussionist.

Publishing a calendar is a terrific way to start the simplification process but defining a cadence that sets the pace for that calendar is where the magic starts happening.

Each month of our life is made of more than 2.5 million component parts we call seconds. If each of those seconds had a random duration, the amount of mental energy it would take to track our progress would increase significantly and could be the cause of major stress and anxiety. Imagine that you have an appointment at noon but you're not exactly sure if the amount of time you have between the current time (say, 11 am) is going to be the equivalent of 3,600 evenly spaced seconds, or if some of those seconds might be equivalent to five seconds, or if on average the time was equivalent to 60 seconds for each one second. What makes time so valuable and allows it to play such a significant role in our lives (without requiring much brain power) is that it is consistent and predictable.

A study published in 2016 in *Nature Communications* and summarized in *The Guardian* by Marc Lewis found that "uncertainty is even more stressful than knowing something bad is definitely going to happen."[10] When we create uncertainty for our team—even when the uncertainty is intended to be something we think will help their business—we increase their stress levels and our business becomes complex or difficult for them.

You create cadence in your organization by committing to a pattern of doing business... a pattern of communications. Be

---

[10] https://www.theguardian.com/commentisfree/2016/apr/04/uncertainty-stressful-research-neuroscience, accessed November 12, 2019.

consistent about when and how often you will launch new programs, and how and how often you will recognize and reward your team. For example, a promotion cadence might mean that you will offer a promotion on the first Monday of each month and it will expire on Wednesday that same week. Your calendar would not reveal what that promotion would be, but the fact that its coming can be published. If it happens consistently the same day of the month or every X days/months, then it is part of your business cadence.

A great example of using cadence for incentives is the practice of announcing a leadership incentive every January at a "leaders only" event and an incentive for all sellers at the summer annual convention. Again, the field knows that there will be a new incentive announced twice a year and when and where that announcement will take place, but they are surprised by the prize or location of the incentive trip.

Not only does a predictable company cadence reduce the stress levels of your team and make them feel like doing business with you is simple, but teams with a strong cadence will reduce costs associated with constantly rushing to meet short deadlines.

Communication

When I joined Origami Owl and had the chance to listen to leaders for the first time, I was surprised to hear them express their disappointment in the company's poor communication. I was surprised because I knew the company was engaging multiple channels of communication and it felt like we were communicating all the time. As I pushed these leaders to try to better understand their concerns, it became clear that it wasn't the *quantity* of communication that was the problem but the lack of a communication cadence. The field didn't necessarily need more information, but they were always afraid that they would miss something. In other words, we might launch a new program on our Facebook page one week and announce a new product on our YouTube channel the next. Leaders wanted to know exactly when and where to tune in for each type of communication. They didn't want to be responsible for monitoring every channel the company was using.

Your team should have a communication system that includes a cadence or frequency of communication. A great communication system starts by answering the questions:

1. **"What do we communicate?"** Things like training, inspirational stories, policy changes, new products, promotions, advancements and recognition, etc.
2. **"Who do we communicate with?"** You will find that some information is suitable for general release, some should be communicated first to your leaders and then from them to their teams, and

other information is better communicated only to leaders. Getting clarity about the type of information that goes to your separate audiences and building a plan for each audience is best practice.

3. **"When and how frequently should we communicate?"** Again, this question could be broken down by content (examples listed above) but should also have built in "opportunity." For example, one of Walmart's competitive advantages is a shift meeting they hold for employees of each department at the beginning of each shift. Walmart doesn't always have critical content to share in the shift meetings every day, yet the meetings have become an advantage because when they do have time sensitive information to relay, they already have a mechanism in place to ensure all employees receive it from a trusted source within 24 hours.

So, as you plan your cadence with your team, make sure you build in some flexibility and have a mechanism in place that allows you a method of communicating with them on short notice (probably not every 24 hours).

4. **"What channel will you use to communicate?"** We have so many options for

communication today. From video conferencing to text messaging to good old-fashioned telephone conferencing to newsletters... you'll find that your team has preferences. You might choose different channels for different messages and that might be driven in part by the audience (e.g. senior leaders vs. all team members). Whichever channel you choose is important, but even more important is to be consistent in using that channel to communicate specific types of information.

We never truly arrive at simple. As your team grows and adds new markets, the fight to keep things simple becomes more and more complex. However, during a turnaround, simplification can help focus resources to improve execution and eliminate programs that are a drain on cash.

Working with Corporate Simplification Efforts

As is the case for many of the elements of our C.H.I.S.E.L. turnaround formula, the simplification process can be unsettling to a field that does not understand what is happening. While improved communication, an annual calendar and a predictable cadence can help field leaders and will be warmly welcomed, other decisions made by companies to simplify things (reducing the number of products, having fewer promotions or new products, etc.) could be troubling. The first role field leaders can play is to effectively lead their team and reassure them that the company is making the best decisions.

Field leaders can lead simplification efforts for their team by aligning with the company's calendar, cadence and communication... if it has one. Here are a few specific do's and don'ts:

- **DON'T create your own programs if the company already has something**. I'm always surprised when leaders add their own team promotions and incentives on top of company programs. On occasion these can be helpful, but for the most part they are a waste of the leader's time and money and create complexity for everyone involved.

- **DO create a communication system for your team...** and modify it as necessary to make sure it doesn't overlap with the company's communication. This can be particularly helpful if your company hasn't yet simplified communication. If you (with the help of other leaders on your team) can summarize communication and make it easy for your team, do it. Also, follow the counsel given to companies above by having a system for your team that includes a way to communicate with leaders, new sellers, the entire team, and those who are part of "push groups" to achieve specific volume or advancement goals.

- **DO be vocal about supporting company decisions to simplify.** As a leader, it is not enough to passively be "OK" with something. During times of doubt and uncertainty good leaders don't remain silent and allow the negative voices to have the floor. Take the proverbial microphone and make sure your team hears about the good and has information to overcome the naysayers that will surely try and grab attention during these times of change.

Chapter 9: Expanding to New Markets—*Finding New Customers in New Places*

The more that you learn, the more places you'll go.
~ Dr. Seuss

When most think about expansion, they think of *international* expansion. I want to broaden your thinking beyond international expansion and encourage you to consider the many domestic expansion opportunities. Most have the opportunity to find new customers for their products in their own country. New domestic markets could include new geographies (cities or states), new demographics (retirees or generation Z) and new languages (e.g. U.S. Chinese speakers). The goal is to find new customers in new places that create new opportunities for your team to pursue.

When we think of international expansion, we think of Amway, Nu Skin, Jeunesse Global, Avon and other household names. When we think of domestic expansion some of the best examples of Renewal from new U.S. markets include:

- ***Melaleuca***—As Melaleuca grew from $20 million to $100 million and then to $200 million, the company did so by tapping into pockets of growth in Minnesota, Orlando and eventually New England. Each of these geographic pockets was essentially a new market and each grew when the company found and supported a new field leader.

- ***Princess House***—One of the waves of growth experienced by Princess House included growth in the U.S. Hispanic market for the first time.

- ***Herbalife***—Technically, they developed the model for their U.S. Hispanic growth in Mexico, but Herbalife saw renewed growth when they introduced Nutrition Clubs to the U.S. Hispanic market.

- ***Jafra***—Again, the success of the U.S. market was no doubt aided by their foreign Spanish speaking countries, but Jafra's U.S. business saw renewed growth when they effectively grew within the U.S. Hispanic market.

- *Amway*—Amway tapped into an entirely new demographic when it first partnered with Energy Drink manufacturer XS (founded by a former Amway distributor) in 2003 and later purchased XS in 2015. In their press release announcing the acquisition, Amway's Chairman Steve Van Andel said, "According to our research, no demographic is more positive about entrepreneurship than those younger than 35, which is the precise target group for the XS brand."[11]

Whether your goal is to discover geographic areas where you have yet to find customers, to expand your reach to a new age segment or to offer your products to customers in the U.S. who prefer to do business in a language other than English, the goal is to identify and develop a strategy to reach customers you're currently not serving.

Domestic Geographic Expansion

A few years ago, I participated in a company's strategic planning process as a partner to one of the world's leading strategy consulting firms. We were asked to prepare a five-year strategic plan for a large U.S.-based direct selling company. As

---

[11] https://www.amwayglobal.com/amway-acquires-xs-energy-brand/ accessed on Sept 30, 2019.

you would expect, the consulting firm went through an extensive evaluation and data analysis before they came back with five strategic recommendations. According to their report, the recommendation with the best return on investment was a campaign to focus on white space opportunities in the United States... this despite the fact that the company had yet to start any international expansion. In other words, they showed how the company had grown in a few key states in the South and Midwest and showed that capturing a similar "fair share" of category sales in other states would more than double sales.

Here are specific tactics field leaders can deploy with their team to find new domestic markets:

(1) Nurture minorities of all types—Make sure your team is a welcome place for all and that you recognize how difficult it can be to be the "first" to join an organization. When you have your "first" Australian or first Chinese person join your team, reach out to them, ask them how you can help them and do all you can to support their efforts—especially if they are recruiting others and request your help.

(2) Be purposeful—*"I'm looking to expand my business to X"*—Ask for referrals and let people know you are looking for team members who speak French or have lived in New Zealand.

(3) *Follow your warm market*—Referrals from your warm market will end up being the strongest team members for you and will in the end be the best way for you to expand to new markets. Ask for referrals and expect that your business will grow through your network and not through cold acquaintances.

(4) *Make a list (launch your business from scratch)*—So many field leaders were taught to start their business by creating a list of people they know. This simple exercise eludes them when they decide to start building their international business. When you begin your business, start from scratch and create a list of people who have lived or done business in a country and another list of those with language capability. Then start working that list and expanding it via referrals from those on the list.

When business has slowed and you can't figure out how to generate new sales from your current customers/distributors, it is time to begin to look for and plan for opportunities to expand. Whether your plans call for expansion into new states or new language markets, finding new customers and creating new opportunities for your distributors to grow their business is a tried and true method of Renewal.

International Expansion

It is true that most direct sellers have plenty of upside opportunity in the U.S., but it is crucial for executives to understand one fact: NO direct selling company has reached and sustained a billion dollars in sales in the United States alone (some have more than a billion now, but I don't know of any that didn't expand beyond the U.S. first). Even some of the largest companies have found it difficult to sustain $500 million in U.S. sales over a long period of time. If you choose to bet on a U.S.-only strategy, realize that you risk losing momentum if your company is growing with sales north of $600 million.

During my tenure at USANA, we had one of the channel's most successful international executives, Bradford Richardson, leading our international expansion efforts. Under his leadership, I played only a supporting role in international expansion, but I had a chance to learn from his success. Bradford led the international business for both USANA Health Sciences and later Shaklee. At both of these companies, he showed how valuable international expansion can be to a direct selling company.

While at USANA we were able to use pricing to renew the distributors' belief in the company, but had we not started on the path of global expansion about the same time, we would have not experienced the long-term growth the company has had over the past two decades. International expansion is a key component to long-term growth in direct selling and often companies err in being too aggressive or too slow to pursue it. I've seen companies wait too long before they expand to new markets and they miss out on the benefit of momentum. Expanding during a company's momentum years is beneficial for both the company and for distributors who have greater cash flow available during those periods to personally invest in building their business in new international markets. Likewise, some companies make the decision to open several (sometimes a dozen or more) new markets in as many months and find themselves with lots of new costs and little new business.

International Expansion for Field Leaders

Field leaders are a key ingredient to the success of any expansion and especially when opening new markets. Field leaders should recognize these new international markets as opportunities to grow their business several times its current size and therefore should consider these new markets as a business investment. Leaders who invest their time and money in new markets are more likely to reap the benefits of these markets. Here are some of the tactics successful international field leaders employ to make the most of expansion:

- *Invest Your Time in New Markets*—Today so much can be done via conference call, video conferencing and social media, but the most successful international leaders invest dedicated and meaningful time in each new market. Prospects and up-and-coming leaders need to have in-person time and enough of it to make sure they can become self-sufficient.

- *Systems for Building In-Market Leadership*—Sometimes leaders can "do it all" for their team in the United States, but time zones, language and distance combine to make it impossible for them to effectively nurture and grow a team in a foreign country. Only those who have a commitment to and system for developing local leaders will see their team grow and develop in a new foreign market.

- *Cultural Education*—Taking time to learn as much as possible about the country and its culture will go a long way in gaining the trust and loyalty of a team in a foreign country.

- *Sponsoring High in the Social Status*—Leaders who are able to attract respected citizens of a foreign country are likely to have more success than starting out by sponsoring the working class. In many countries (especially in Asia), class matters more than in the U.S., and recruiting up is so much more difficult than starting with professionals and expanding from there. Take the time to network with and begin your efforts high in the country's ranks of social status.

- *Growing in Your Market First*—As soon as your company announces a new market, I would immediately begin to try and find those with in-country and/or language experience. For example, if you are going to Japan, start by finding Japanese speakers and Japanese living in the U.S.

- *Support the Company Even if You Don't Go*—Even if your current situation doesn't allow you to grow your team in a new market, the company's success in that market can benefit you directly when someone on your team recruits someone from that country, or indirectly by making your company more financially stable or making your opportunity more attractive to other potential distributors.

RENEWAL for Field Leaders

Chapter 10: Leading During Tough Times—

Being Present and Positive

A good leader doesn't get stuck behind a desk.

~ Richard Branson

George Washington is without peer in human history. He was the first to lead a colonial army to victory, the first to become the undisputed leader of the newly conquered country and then, at his own insistence, to voluntarily limit his term of office and step aside so that there would be a second president of the United States of America. Those who met Washington in his years as General of the Continental Army said that there was never a man more fitted for his role in history than he.

When Washington took command of the ragtag group of volunteer militia that he would later label the "Continental

Army," he was humbled by the trust the Continental Congress had put in him and eager to prove worthy of that trust. However, he had no idea how ill-prepared his men were to fight. It took them eight days to produce a simple count of the men under his command. His army had no uniforms, few reliable guns, and a woefully small amount of gunpowder available.

Washington and his army camped for months with nothing to show for their efforts. They were at a standstill with the British and neither side was willing to risk an offensive. Despite Washington's urging, the Generals that made up his "Counsel on War" refused to support him when on four separate occasions he petitioned them with a proposal to attack the British.

In December 1775, the contracts of most of his army expired and thousands returned to their homes rather than wait out a New England winter as soldiers for a stalled army. During this time, Washington, the man who would go down in history as of one of the finest leaders in the world, lamented in a private letter to a friend:

> *The reflection upon my situation and that of this army produces many an uneasy hour, when all around me are wrapped in sleep. Few people know the predicament that we are in. There is too little powder. Still no money.*

Washington, like many a leader before and after him, was discouraged and took this moment in history—months before the Declaration of Independence would be penned and signed—to feel sorry for himself and to wish he had never taken on the role of leader. He wrote:

> *I have often thought how much happier I should have been if instead of accepting of a command under such circumstances, I had taken my musket upon my shoulders and entered the ranks, or if I could have justified the measure to posterity, and my own conscience, and I had retired to the back country and lived in a wigwam. If I shall be able to rise superior to these and many other difficulties which might be enumerated, I shall most religiously believe that the finger of Providence is upon us.*

Leadership—especially in difficult times—is not easy and many a leader like the great George Washington has no doubt wished that they could hide or that they never would have become a leader in the first place. It is in these times that one must be conscious of the natural tendency we have to shrink and wish to lead from a safe place.

Too often, when teams are struggling, I have counseled with leaders who have stopped doing all of the things that led to success in the past. They reduced or eliminated team meetings, stopped traveling (citing a lack of funds to pay for travel expenses) and opted to use email and other forms of written communication to fulfill their responsibilities.

It is during these times, when everything in us wants to be behind a desk, that we most need to be with and lead our teams. It is OK not to have the answer to your current problems, but it is not OK to hope that the answer will come to you as if by magic. You must strike out and find the answers to the question "How will we renew growth?" Even during times when you can't articulate the path forward, you can articulate your vision of what is possible and have confidence that if you speak your vision often enough, some listener will believe sufficiently to blaze the way forward.

You need to be ever present in times of decline. You need to continue to:

- ***Find and recognize those who are having success!***
- ***Tell your story***—the story of your future and your vision for what your team can be to the world.

- ***Be listening and learning***—In person to those who are having challenges and especially to those who are having success.

- ***Be Honest***—About where you are and about your determination to work with your team to find your way back to growth.

- ***Be Hopeful***—You need to muster the inner strength and find reasons to have hope. Hope cannot be faked. It won't work unless you actually are filled with hope.

Whether you are a corporate leader or a field leader there are activities you should begin during good times and continue during tough times to make sure you are able to lead your team to Renewal and growth. These activities include:

- **Make Your Team Sticky**—Great leaders make others feel like they are part of something and that they are committed to something bigger than themselves. They make it hard for others to leave by making sure others feel that there are people on the team who care personally about their success.

- **Communicate Through Challenges**—Tough times bring opportunities for tough talks or the risk of strained relationships. Milan Jensen, founder of Womenkind, is one of the world's great connectors. She has worked magic with field leaders who seemed to dislike one another so much that others had given up on them. Milan described for me a session she once led with the leaders of a small company. As the company was executing a plan for renewal, the top leaders, including the founder, were concerned that one of the original leaders was becoming more and more disengaged. There was a noticeable decline in her enthusiasm, she stopped contributing ideas, and she vocalized feeling disconnected from the vision of the company. The solution was to bring this small group together in a safe environment with the intention and commitment of creating unity.

Milan told me about a day of sharing that seemed to come to a head when the leader who had been struggling shared her fears and disappointments, and rather than defend or blame, the others listened. They asked her to help them understand why she felt the way she did. By the end of the day, the leader who was at risk for being "on her way out" now felt the value of their unity and tearfully said, "I never wanted to leave." She just wanted to be heard. Together they committed to restoring trust and unity with each other. During tough times, learning to both listen and share are essential skills for effective leaders.

- **Be Free with Your Grace**—While I am offering you a formula with variables that should be part of your turnaround efforts, I'm not offering a guaranteed plan and I have had both amazing success and very public failures in my efforts to lead turnarounds. Turnarounds are tough and assuredly there will be mistakes made along the way. Field leaders need to expect and allow for failed company programs and resist the urge to blame the management team for the decline.

  Likewise, corporate leaders need to understand that most periods of Hyper-Growth promote unprepared individuals into leadership positions they are not fully equipped to execute flawlessly. Both company and field leaders need to be offered grace, time and resources to help them figure out the business challenges they are suddenly forced to solve during the Shake-Out stage.

- **Be Present**—Your team needs to see you, hear from you and be in rooms with you—now more than ever. As much as your insecurity about your new reality may leave you wanting to be alone, it is during these tough times that your teams need you... live. As tight as cash can be, you must make other cuts to allow you to maintain money to invest in being present.

Should you risk being in public if you don't have any answers? YES! Showing up just to assure your team that you're on the job "figuring things out" is so much more valuable to your company than your absence and the fertile ground that creates for your team's greatest fears to flourish like yet-to-be-pulled weeds.

- **Invest in Yourself and Your Team**—If you ask network marketing expert Eric Worre, he will tell you that often Hyper-Growth stalls and decline follows because a company grew faster than its ability to grow its leadership. With too few leaders, sales must correct itself by declining to match the level of leadership. If this is the case, then those in leadership—both in the field and in the company—owe it to their teams to invest in their personal development and to learn as much and as fast as they can to improve their ability to lead. Great leaders will read books, listen to lectures and hire experienced advisors to help them accelerate their growth and fill in for the blindness their inexperience often brings.

A Rational Look at "Irrational" Field Fears

I want to end this chapter with one of the most important lessons of my career and one that forever changed my relationship with those with whom I have worked in the field. During times of sales decline, it is easy for corporate leaders to be surprised by feelings of intense mistrust and anger from field leaders who have previously been so positive. I experienced this early in my career when one of the leaders I respected the most began to show and express deep mistrust and doubt about most of the proposals the corporate team proposed. My initial reaction was to label her "ungrateful," but I knew inside that was not true. One afternoon I drove to meet with her and her husband in their home and in that environment, with no verbal instruction, I learned the following lesson...

For those of us with a corporate salary, it is fairly easy to make a career change and expect to replace and perhaps even improve our income. It is not that simple for field leaders. Those who have built a large sales team and earned a sizeable income from scratch don't have the opportunity to take that team to another company and replace that income elsewhere (I realize some companies promise that to leaders but in reality, it rarely happens). The idea of rebuilding another sales team seems impossible—or at the very least, not desirable.

These top leaders begin to realize how dependent they are on the company they represent and the management of that company. They realize that their earnings can be significantly impacted by things completely out of their control. Given this anxiety, many top leaders become more risk averse for fear that any changes made by the company could significantly impact their income and lifestyle. This trepidation often is interpreted by management as being "negative" or "emotional" rather than "grateful" and "logical."

Field leaders should recognize the psychology of their position and avoid allowing their fears to go unchecked and express themselves in aggressive and negative behavior to corporate leadership... and especially, to impact the hope and confidence of their team. I have found that fear is best overcome with service that will strengthen your relationships within the corporate team. Take them to lunch. Send them personal cards. Recognize, appreciate and praise the company throughout the organization. Your team will also be inspired by the example you set of creating unity with the company.

Chapter 11: Beyond Your C.H.I.S.E.L.—*Other Considerations That Impact Pace*

Perspective is worth 80 IQ points.
~ Alan Kay, Scientist

While the variables we have introduced make up the core ingredients of a successful turnaround, employing them effectively requires context and perspective. I have learned through sad experience that organizations, precisely because of the humans that compose them, need much attention and attentiveness to their attitude and disposition in order to reach their full potential.

Change Fatigue

For Christmas in 2016 my wife convinced me to surprise our youngest daughter with a dog that she had "earned" and I had tried in vain to avoid. The video of her uncontrollable joy and tender tear-filled reception of a little four-pound Morkie (Maltese/Yorkie mix) by the name of Jack went viral over the next few days,[12] and in spite of my reluctance, I became a bit of a folk hero for my part in acquiring this new pet. That would not be the end of my role because Jack decided that I would be his Alpha. On most days he follows me around begging me to take him for a walk or give him a treat. Even with his zealous begging for a walk, I have found on several occasions that Jack's enthusiasm for walking often ends before my intended route is complete. Jack has learned to abandon his spot in front leading me along the path and instead take up a position between my feet, making it almost impossible for me to walk. When I look down, he looks up and I've now been trained to pick him up and carry him the rest of the way home.

Our organizations can be a lot like Jack. Even though they are excited and aware of the need to hurry through the trail of tough times, the team's stamina doesn't always keep pace with that of their leaders. A wise leader will recognize when it is necessary to put things on pause, slow the pace, or find a way to give team members a rest.

A wise leader recognizes that change fatigue is real and that sometimes the pace for the way forward needs to be recalibrated. This is a good perspective for leaders of turnarounds to have.

---

[12] https://youtu.be/BlKpTKO4UHo

Self-care

As you embark on a turnaround, you will need the support of those close to you and you will need to be disciplined about caring for your mental, emotional and physical health. Turnarounds are draining. Most often they are marathons that require you to run at sprint-like speed. Not only can they take a toll on your physical health, but they can introduce significant stress into the life of your family (spouse and children). They strain all of your relationships as you are forced to spend more time at work and on the road.

Hire a coach or a team of coaches to help you through the challenges of your life and business. Don't expect yourself to be an expert in every area of life. Recognize the value of receiving help and support from experts who have been down this road that is so foreign to you now. Take vacation—a minimum of two weeks a year and preferably one week a quarter. Yes, I'm recommending that you take *more* time for yourself and your family, even during those times when your business seems to need you the most. You might be pleasantly surprised at how quickly the answers to your toughest business challenges come when your mind is in vacation mode rather than nonstop crisis management mode.

Get Creative at Celebration

The fatigue of always seeing a falling scorecard can be overwhelming to you and your team. Every team wants to win. Finding meaningful and realistic milestones and successes you can celebrate will require creativity and mindfulness. In other words, train yourself and your team to establish milestones you are likely to be able to celebrate and to be on the lookout for things worth celebrating. Then... take the time to celebrate them!

Chapter 12: When You Fail to Renew—*Other Options When Growth Doesn't Happen*

Success is not final; failure is not fatal.
~ Winston Churchill

Several years ago, I received a call from an investor who had an interest in a direct selling company that at one point had sales of several hundred million dollars. This company had seen sales decline to $150 million and the private equity owner had decided to liquidate it at all costs. This investor had the chance to purchase the company for pennies on the dollar and came to me with the question, "If you were me, would you buy this company?"

I met with the current management team, reviewed the financials, product offering and history, and a few weeks later called the investor to report that I would not make the purchase. He was surprised but patient and followed my advice. A few days later the company was sold for less than $20 million to another direct seller who would make the products available but who really wanted the field leaders that were still left.

I concluded that this company was beyond Renewal and that it was unlikely it would ever regain growth because of the shaky foundation and lack of discipline the field had experienced. I'm not sure my decision was correct, but it is not the only time in my life I've come to a similar conclusion, and not the only company I've seen in similar straits. In fact, just as I set out to write this book, I had a call with the owner of a company that was producing sales of just 20% of what it had been producing two years earlier. This company also had debt. The founder's question to me was, "How much do you think I could sell the company for?" My answer was a disappointing amount, much less than the debt owed at the time.

The sad reality is that sometimes, businesses fail. Not all of them can be saved. Some, like Herbalife, will survive the Shake-Out stage and others, like Longaberger, will not.[13] We have given you a set of tools and advice to help ensure that your team experiences Renewal rather than failure, but if it does not show

---

[13] Ironically, just as we are preparing to publish this book the Longaberger family is attempting to relaunch the company starting with an appearance on QVC.

signs of revitalization, what are your options? What should you do?

Maintain a long-term view

As Winston Churchill stated, "Failure is not fatal" and even though you may lose the company you are leading now, it doesn't mean your business life is over. Yesterday I had a very exciting phone call with the founder of a company that was off to an impressive start. He had attracted notable investors, a strong board and excellent field leaders to help him launch his second direct selling company after his first was forced to close a few years ago. As you make decisions about your business, do so with a long-term view in mind and with the expectation that the choices you make will have an impact on your future. While the company you represent may not always be around your relationships can endure if you focus on always developing others. In other words, whatever you do, act with class

Finding Your "Next"

No matter what a company decides to do, field leaders have their own decision to make if and when their company doesn't make it or perhaps when their income falls below a sustainable level. Those who were earning full-time income may decide to fill in their loss with a part-time or full-time job, or they may decide that it is time to go in a different direction altogether. If you are a field leader looking for a new company, let me offer you some suggestions for what to look for and what to avoid, but first a few words of advice:

- ***Speed vs. Resolve*—**While you may feel pressure to find something fast, especially if you risk losing your team to another company, don't let speed trump resolve. In other words, don't join a company just because you feel like you don't have time to find something better. Building a direct selling business is difficult, even when you bring the strength of a team that has worked together in the past. But it is excruciatingly painful when you realize you're building a business for a company that doesn't share your values or whose product you don't love. If forced to choose to go fast or to wait for the right thing—wait.

- ***Test, then Scale*—**Don't be afraid to test a company you think will be great. Try the product, even try selling and sponsoring for a few weeks, but if you discover along the way that the product or company is not all you hoped for, DO NOT SETTLE. It is perfectly OK to switch companies a few days, weeks or even months into a "next company" experience. In the end you will be so, so happy that you had the integrity to find the right fit. Once you've fallen in love with your new company and feel it's a good match, go fast and hard and scale your business.

"I just couldn't do it!"

Recently I received a call from a former employee who was so excited about her first VP role in a company that was growing and well known. She asked a few questions and we ended the conversation with her voice full of energy. Less than two months later, this same friend called back and sheepishly described the short tenure she had at the company she'd been so excited about initially. She said, "Brett, when I learned the truth about the CEO and her values, I just couldn't stay."

Perhaps she thought I would think less of her, but I thought more highly of her than ever before and we went to work together to find a fit she felt great about.

Finding a New Home—What to Look For

When it is time to find a new home, here are the things I would look for if I were joining a company as a field leader:

- **Product Fit**—I don't think anything else matters as much. If you aren't in love with the product and excited about using it every day for the rest of your life, this is not the company for you.

- **Culture/Value Fit**—Often you can't really understand the values and culture of a company in the interview process, but you can ask values-based questions and you can look to see if they are attracting others who share your same values. Even if you find out after you join, run away as fast as you can if you find a company whose values are not in tune with your own. Milan Jensen reminds leaders that "culture outweighs vision every time. It's much more important to align with a company's culture than it is to fall in love with their mission. People may be attracted by what they hear, however they will stay based on how they feel."

- **Customer Focus**—In today's regulatory and social environment, if your company is "opportunity focused" and not consumer or product focused, I don't believe you will last. In my opinion, the only sustainable model for direct sellers requires that they focus on selling products to consumers, and then converting delighted customers into distributors.

- **Momentum**—If you are forced to look for a second company, momentum should matter to you. Avoid those who are reaching the peak of Hyper-Growth (three to five years into it) and those in a decline. Instead, look for companies that are just experiencing growth or even better, those who have been through Hyper-Growth and are experiencing Renewal and growth after a period of flattening or decline.

- **Systems**—Your chance of success is much greater if the company or the team you are joining has proven systems for attracting customers, upgrading customers to distributors, on-boarding distributors, helping distributors get to profitability, and developing leaders. Having all those systems in place is the ideal, but at the very least having an excellent customer acquisition system is essential.

- **Consumable Products**—While your passion might be jewelry or vacuums or cookware, history has proven that your direct selling business is likely to be more successful over time if the products you sell are consumable and lend themselves to frequent reorders. Even better, if your company has a consumer friendly (not comp plan friendly) subscription program, your job as a distributor will be so much easier.

- **Management Team**—Management that shows a commitment to doing the right thing for the right reason is essential. Too many direct selling executives have become celebrities in their own company, and they make decisions that preserve their popularity at the expense of running a great business. If the executives leading your company are leading the life of a celebrity, chances are they are not making decisions that will ensure long-term viability for you. Keep looking until you find a management team that clearly cares about their field.

Corporate Opportunities

Through the years, I have heard from several top field leaders who want to trade in their upside for steady. In other words, they want to become corporate employees for direct selling companies and are willing to trade in the benefits of being a distributor.

Here are the quick answers to the most frequently asked questions of those thinking about a corporate job:

- ***How much can I earn?*** Most former distributors enter corporations in regional sales manager positions which pay anywhere from $45k to $80k (a few may find pay up to $150K) depending on the amount of travel required and the size of the company. These positions typically have a bonus program that would be anywhere from 5-15% of the base salary.

- ***Can I work from home?*** Often you can work from home, but typically the company will require you to travel to their headquarters at least once a quarter and many require you to travel throughout your region every week.

- ***Where can I find opportunities?*** There are a few search firms that specialize in direct selling that you will want to connect with. You can search the supplier portal of the Direct Selling Association website. I have also seen a list published on the Social Selling News website.[14] You should also reach out to corporate

---

[14] https://socialsellingnews.com/the-ranks/executive-search-firms/

executives you know, especially those who are working for a company different than the one you now sell for. On occasion companies will publish positions on their website. Most CEOs and founders, especially of small companies, are open to a cold call—especially if you have studied their company and have passion and enthusiasm for working for them.

- ***Pros and cons***—The pros of working for a direct selling company are that you will have a steady and predictable paycheck and the chance to share what you have learned with others. Many regional sales representatives find it rewarding to help others succeed and they enjoy the chance to coach and speak and travel (often they attend company incentive trips).

  The cons of working for a company are that it is more difficult to significantly change your earnings and to measure the direct impact of the work you are doing. You're recognizing others more and often being recognized yourself less. And then there's corporate politics, which are real and can impact your career and job satisfaction significantly.

Acknowledgments

I wish to acknowledge and express my gratitude for the dozens of executives, consultants and friends who have contributed content to this book. The direct selling industry is unique in the warm relationships executives have with one another and I have been blessed with many, many close friends.

I'm especially grateful for Milan Jensen, CEO and founder of Womenkind, for helping me lead a discussion on *Renewal* with several bright and accomplished executives.

I'm grateful for my editor, Pamela Suarez, for her amazing work and her skill in helping me improve my finished product considerably. I'm also grateful for Stuart Johnson, CEO of SUCCESS Partners and his team who provided valuable insight and assistance in getting the book published and in helping me find an audience that can benefit from its contents.

Finally, a special thanks for the love, support and patience of my wife and eternal companion, Erin, whom I love, and our children: Spencer and his wife Maris (the parents of our first grandson, Brooks), Madison, Allison, Sydney and Kate, and to my father and friend Dr. Leon H. Blake.

About the Author

Brett A. Blake is a direct selling veteran having led four companies (both person-to-person and party plan), served as a marketing executive for two others and served on several boards. He has served as the president, CEO or GM of seven companies, both public and private. He is the author of ***Private Equity Investing in Direct Selling: Identifying Risks & Rewards***, and ***RENEWAL: Leading Direct Selling Turnarounds.*** Brett is a Partner with The ServiceQuest Group, where he leads Renewal Strategy Sessions for corporate executives and top field leaders. He is one of the most experienced turnaround executives in direct selling, having led turnaround efforts at five companies. Brett is a personal advisor and coach to CEOs, boards and investors.

In addition to writing and speaking to company executives and field leaders, Brett enjoys mountain biking and spending time with his wife Erin, their six children (one by marriage) and their newborn grandson. Brett will leave his consulting and speaking work beginning in July 2020, because he, Erin and their youngest daughter Kate have been called to lead the Colorado Denver North Mission for the Church of Jesus Christ of Latter-day Saints for three years.

Made in the USA
Columbia, SC
16 February 2021

33055312R00098